WHY READ A WAYNE JACOBSEN BOOK?

"Wayne Jacobsen's books hold and lead you by the hand to meet and then leave you in the company of the best friend you will ever know."

JONATHAN, on a hill in Wales

"Wayne is a regular guy with an extraordinary message—God loves you in a way you can hardly begin to understand even after years of religious practice."

NANCY, a college professor in Georgia

"Even for a missionary kid who grew up in a godly family, his teachings have been a brain explosion, shattering the glass wall that I've been desperately peering through for decades. His teaching has thrust me into the thriving relationship with Christ I've been craving my whole life. If you feel like you have hit a wall with God, get his books. You won't be disappointed!"

GLORY, a missionary kid, now military wife and homeschool mom in Texas

"Wayne puts words to the questions you don't realize you have and allows the Holy Spirit to answer them. He lives what he writes."

HARVEY, a fruit farmer in Ohio

"If you have a fire burning in you that says, 'Something just doesn't feel right about what Christianity looks like today,' you will love Wayne Jacobsen's books."

LAUREN, a birth doula in eastern Tennessee

"For thirteen years, I have watched Wayne live what he teaches as he helps many to navigate the transition from religious obligation into the joy of living loved. His illustrations light up the truths he shares with living color. If 'church-as-usual' leaves you empty and hungry, don't miss reading *Beyond Sundays*."

DAVID, a former pastor, and writer in Oklahoma

"Wayne's storytelling and warm tone welcome many a weary traveler to the throne of Grace. His words are rich with love."

DEREK, a husband, and father to two daughters in New York

"The refining Wayne has been through lends authenticity and credibility to the insight Father has given him, which is built on a solid foundation of increasingly knowing Jesus. Wayne steps away from the limelight to allow the Holy Spirit to take centre stage."

PHILLIP, retired near Cape Town, South Africa

"Wayne causes me to look deeply into my relationship with God and the church and ask why do I believe what I believe. His desire is that all come to know the great affection our Father has for each of us and how that love can change so much in our lives."

KAREN, a mother of five in Roanoke, VA

"When your journey takes you outside the walls of church-as-usual, you look around to see if you are as alone as you feel. Someone walks up to you, smiles and says: 'I have been where you are. You are okay. Let me walk alongside you for a while.' Meet Wayne Jacobsen—his wisdom, his passion and his stories will help your transition from a life defined by religion to the most amazing 'God Journey' you've ever been on."

RUBY, a poet and pilgrim in Alberta

"I was a pastor for eight years and often wondered if there was something beyond the stained-glass experience. Wayne Jacobsen articulated to me in his books and teachings what the true, biblical reality of 'church' really is."

JAMES, a former pastor and medical security officer in North Carolina

"Most of my life I feel I have been in a constant audition. Wayne's writings have helped me to understand that I have always had the part."

DENNIS, a husband and father in Georgia

"We were so grateful to God for directing us to Wayne's books because he put into words the things that God had been teaching us, and we realised we weren't all alone after all."

DAVID and SUE, grandparents to seven in England!

"Whether you are inside or outside the walls of an organized institution Wayne will send you on a journey to discover and develop your personal relationship with the Father and Son."

LINDSEY, a home educator in Oklahoma

"Having been in the institution for over twenty years, deeply indoctrinated and full of despair, I found myself mentally broken. Someone recommended *He Loves Me*, which led me to contact Wayne. He graciously met with me and my husband and answered my questions with patience and kindness. He is one of the spiritually safest men I have ever met. You are reading someone who genuinely knows how to live in the love of the Father."

GADIELA, a mother under deconstruction in Southern California

"Every book by Wayne has been a refreshing shower of life that washes away the grime of dead religion, beckoning me into a deeper relationship with my Father. See for yourself!"

JOEL, a husband and father of four in Bailey, NC

"Wayne is a man with his feet on earth and his heart in heaven. What he writes is real, practical and filled with love from our heavenly Daddy as if a friend is talking to you."

EDWIN and ELLEMIEKE, The Hague, The Netherlands

"In the midst of all the religiosity Wayne will help you find the gentle and loving face of Jesus again smiling at you and welcoming you home. And back in his arms you will be able to breathe freely again."

KIRSTEN, a social worker in Germany

"Wayne doesn't cling to lofty theories of what could be. Rather he writes of a reality he actually lives. Reading a book by Wayne is like reading a letter from an older brother saying, 'Here's some stuff I've experienced in my journey with Father that may encourage you.'"

LOREN, NBC Broadcast Operations in Texas

"We have been refreshingly changed in so many ways by Wayne's books, and have shared what we have learned with friends and family in our community who have also been impacted by his words. He brings a message of freedom, hope and grace to those who are tired of the insanity of living religiously and desperately wanting to express Jesus in their daily life!"

GREG and KIM, parents and grandparents in Arizona

"Wayne is a creative thinker who reaches out to anyone seeking a relational understanding of who God is and what it means to be part of the body of Christ. His perspective and humanity has invited me to ask the hard questions and connect relationally with God who loves me."

ALISA, a special education teacher in Virginia

"Wayne has helped me over many years come to grips with my dissatisfaction and to see relationship is more important than religion."

MARSHALL, 60, a father of five in Louisiana

"After reading *So You Don't Want to Go to Church Anymore* I knew I had found my new favorite author. Wayne Jacobsen is a guy I don't want to follow, but want to befriend. His writing is the cool cup of water for a Christ follower."

SHANNON, a pastor's wife in the South

"Wayne's presentation of the life of Jesus has been like that of an unassuming, close friend that is happy to sit with you in the dark places of your life, and firmly but gently point you to Jesus. The result is a return to wonder, and peace of mind and heart. Wayne's role in my life, through his books, has been deeply influential."

JOHN, a fellow traveler from Alberta

"Sometimes you're not as lost as you think; you just need a different map."

PATRICK, a public school teacher in Virginia

"Wayne Jacobsen's teaching has been used of God to lead me out of living a dutiful Christian life into an abundant freedom where I know how much I am loved by the Father. That is life-changing."

DEB, a fifty-year-old, life-embracing Australian woman

"Wayne isn't one to control or guilt you into believing his thoughts about God but trusts God to guide each of us. Gracious in his words, he nonetheless challenges the ways organized religion has missed the message of Jesus."

MIKE, a retired mental health professional in Atlanta, Georgia

"When I discovered *Finding Church*, I was elated to read a book that expressed what I had found so difficult to put into words myself. Wayne gets to the heart of the matter without condemning anyone."

MARGARET, a retired teacher in Florida

"Extreme simplicity and humility are mixed with profound wisdom as Wayne explains God's boundless love, his unattached truth and his liberating message as no one has done in my almost fifty-eight years of life."

PABLO, a pilgrim in Barcelona, Spain

"I picked up a copy of *So You Don't Want to Go to Church Anymore* and found myself in its pages. Wayne has provided those just-on-time words again and again through his books, podcasts and blogs. My focus and purpose have become clear that has begun a ripple effect that touches everyone I come in contact with."

JOYCE from Southern Iowa

"After forty years of being hurt and manipulated by 'churches,' I was done. But leaving didn't make me free. After reading books from Wayne, I am beginning to finally live loved! His books are always must-reads!"

JEFF, a small business owner in Evergreen, CO

"Wayne Jacobsen is a modern-day Martin Luther. As God is leading us beyond Luther's Reformation, Wayne's books provide the map and light to illuminate the path."

LINDA, running from religion in San Diego, CA

"Finally, someone out there understood my frustration with organized religion. Wayne's writings show me that God's not upset with me; he's on this journey *with* me. I can finally enjoy Him in ways I never imagined."

CHRISTINE, a mosquito hunter in Virginia

"I found myself wanting something more than just Sundays. My earthly father abandoned the family when I was five and Wayne helped introduce me to my real Father in such a way that was desirable, understandable, and simple. Beautiful beyond measure!"

JON, one relentlessly sought by God in North Carolina

"I found Wayne at the lowest part of my life. After meeting him personally, and hearing his heart for people, I found his desire to help people find an organic life in Christ genuine. He's having the conversation about what organized religion could be missing."

MIKE, an actor/voice-over artist in Atlanta, GA

"A book by Wayne gives a well-crafted voice to my own journey and breathes life to my soul! He is so down-to-earth and always so 'up-to-Jesus' that I come away encouraged, refreshed and built-up. I usually buy more than one copy, because I know they will be abundantly shared with others."

LORRIE, a sojourner from Canada

"When I read Wayne's books it is as if the glasses I have been looking through to see God have been buffed and polished to crystal clear. I can now see through the fog of religion."

PATTI, a free-ranger in Kansas

"Wayne articulates what the Holy Spirit has already been speaking to me and is a man of great character, even taking the time to answer emails from people he doesn't know. It doesn't get more real and authentic than that."

VICTORIA, a homeschooling mom in small-town Iowa

"I served as a church planter and pastor for nearly twenty years and was quite shocked when my marriage fell apart and I sat alone in depression. Then I was given Wayne's book, *He Loves Me*, and it was as though a bright light turned on in the dark room of my soul. I've finally found the victory of our faith, and it is wonderful!"

TERRY, a brother in Jesus from North Carolina

"Wayne invites us to learn with him as he discovers what it means to live in a love relationship with the Father instead by our own performance. He is a bright, competent, gifted communicator who makes the complex simple as well as connects the dots on *how to* live in the Father's love."

TRACI, a mother of two in Pennsylvania

"A bloke who is down to earth, real about God and the stuff of life. The peace and contentment that emanates in the way Wayne speaks is a place I long to reach in my own walk with God."

BRYR, an Aussie listener to The God Journey podcast

"I was set free from a homosexual lifestyle, but the abandonment of my church in those darkest hours took the longest to heal. God led me to read Wayne's book *He Loves Me*. I experienced God healing old wounds, restoring my trust in godly men and women, and the removal of the guilt and shame. This book paved the way for me to live and make decisions from the heart Jesus gave me."

DANIËL, a former missionary in Cape Town, SA

"Connect to what's real!"   SERGE, a high-tech entrepreneur in Ukraine

"Wayne has been a friend, a big brother, mentor, cheerleader—a living example of coming alongside showing what it means to be part of God's Church. His nutty and funny sarcasm, wit, tenderness and honesty, I can hear him in his writings. Talk about truth in advertising—book Wayne is real-life Wayne. And my kids love him too."

AMY, a wife and mother of two in Central California

"Wayne puts into words things I didn't know I knew!"

HELEN, in the UK

"The first book written by Wayne Jacobsen that popped up in my Kindle had me captivated. Suddenly here was an author who was answering my deepest questions."

RUTH, a grandmother from a country town in Australia

"I met Wayne a few years ago and he is a man who is at home in his own skin—no pretense and oozing with grace. His books have a way of uncovering the truth God is speaking to your heart and he encourages you to live in there."

DAVID, a former pastor in Alabama

"I always, always, learn something from Wayne. He writes of the Father's love and nonreligious notions in a way that brings healing to my heart and allows me to have something to give to others."

DENISE, a middle-school counselor in South Carolina

"I have enjoyed Wayne's podcasts, books, and articles for a number of years. We had a chance to get to know the man behind the books and found him unassuming, real, down to earth, and all about Jesus. He lives what he writes...what a concept!"

PAMELA, a Christ-follower from the Ozarks

"For the past twenty years I have been consistently and greatly encouraged by Wayne Jacobsen through his podcasts, articles and books. I believe he has an ear finely tuned to 'hear what the Spirit is saying to the churches,' and is able to articulate clearly those things that the Spirit is also whispering to others like myself who find themselves half a step behind him!"

SUE, a grandmother and refugee support worker in Western Australia

"When I met him in person he helped me to sort out a dilemma that was weighing heavily on my mind at the time. The solution was simple — it involved God's love, learning to live 'loved' and knowing that we are all loved."

BEV ANNE, a free-range believer on Victoria Island

"Wayne disappears as he lovingly lifts up Jesus into my sight line. I know of no higher compliment. He will not tell you what to believe, or attach your obedience to his vision—a rare leader in this era of Christianity. What he will do, is encourage and enable you to draw closer to God who came to earth to find you, and thus experience true transformation by being utterly loved. I'm so glad to have Wayne as part of my journey."

LISA, a mother of two in Ohio

Beyond SUNDAYS

Why those who are done with religious institutions
can be a blessing for the Church

WAYNE JACOBSEN

Trailview Media
Newbury Park, CA

International Standard Book Number
978-0-9839491-9-0

Trailview Media, an imprint of Lifestream
www.lifestream.org
1560 Newbury Road, Suite 1
Newbury Park, CA 91320
(805) 498-7774
fax: (805) 499-5975
office@lifestream.org

Cover and Interior designs: Nan Bishop, www.nbishopsdesigns.com

Printed in the United States of America
Original Printing February 1, 2018

. . . .

DEDICATION

A few years ago we fell into the lap of some wonderful people from Kenya who had a hunger to discover the Father's love and some profound needs in the wake of tribal violence following a disputed election. Through them a few years ago, we also came in touch with over 100,000 people in North Pocket who were suffering from a prolonged drought, malnutrition, and disease. Many generous readers in my audience responded with love and generosity to send over $1.4 million dollars over seven years to help with orphans, education, medical needs, emergency relief and to plant the seeds for a sustainable economy to take hold in Pokot. In doing so many lives have been touched and a forgotten, nomadic people have come face to face with the Gospel of God's love and have responded with open hearts and great joy.

I dedicate this book to the hundreds of people who have given to my brothers and sisters in Kenya in amounts ranging from $10.00 to $500,000.00, and to the people of Kitale who have been our arms and hearts extended to those people. A light has arisen in the darkness and I am grateful for all those who shared their resource with people they will never meet this side of eternity.

· · · · · · · · · · · ·

CONTENTS

PREFACE

In the last few decades, sixty-five million Americans who once regularly attended a local congregation no longer do. About thirty-five million of those no longer self-identify as Christian, but over thirty-one million still do. This last group has been tagged "The Dones": those who still seek to follow Jesus and find real community, but who have given up hope that the local congregation is still relevant to their journey.

What do we make of this phenomenon? Does it threaten the future of God's work in our world, or does it create new opportunities for God to make himself known, even if it challenges our hopes or preconceptions?

I have spent my life in both places. I grew up in a traditional congregation and pastored in two of them for over twenty years. For the past twenty-three, however, I've spent more time outside with those who no longer participate in a Sunday (or Saturday) morning institution. I see the animosity between the two camps, and I yearn for the day when we can have a healing dialog consistent with the prayer of Jesus that we would all be one. Nothing, he said, would demonstrate his reality better to the world than the love his people share together.

It's a conversation we desperately need, and not just between various factions of Christianity. I hope this book can seed that conversation between friends and families in communities throughout the world. Whether you attend a local church or whether you don't, responding to this phenomenon will have repercussions for generations to come. We can continue to treat each other with suspicion and judgment that further fracture our Father's family, or we can celebrate all the ways he works to bring people to himself and transform them in his love.

Additionally, I hope this book encourages those who have lost their mooring in institutional Christianity and yet still hunger for a relationship with God and real community with others. The failures of organized religion do not discount God's reality or your opportunity to get to know him. I want to help you navigate a life of growing faith and impact in the world beyond the institutional borders that may have harmed you.

This is a propitious moment in Christian history, and all the more so as the world darkens around us. May we all respond in a way that allows the glory of the Lord to arise out of the love of his people, and by doing so, proclaim to the world that our God is real and worthy to be followed.

CHAPTER 1

THE SECRET IS OUT!

One of the best-kept secrets of the faith is that you don't have to be committed to a local congregation to live out a transforming relationship with Jesus, to experience the wonder of Christian community, or to find meaningful ways to extend his kingdom in the world. But of course, our religious institutions have a vested interest in keeping that secret.

We've known for some time that people are leaving traditional congregations in droves. The statistics are irrefutable. Popular wisdom, and no small number of sermons, told us that people who were not part of a congregation are not part of the church. Their salvation is suspect and they will wither away spiritually either because their spiritual passion would wane or they would get lost in the weeds of false teaching. And while that is true of some, researchers have now identified a large group of people who are thriving in their faith beyond the walls of any local congregation.

Dr. Josh Packard and Ashleigh Hope call them "The Dones," in their book *Church Refugees*, published in 2015. The book is subtitled, "Sociologists reveal why people are DONE with church but not their faith" and helps us to understand this heretofore unidentified group of believers. They describe the Dones as high-capacity people, who were deeply involved in their local fellowships until they become stifling to their own journey. For years they sought to help reform it, only to find their efforts and their passion stifled by a bureaucracy that resisted change. Finally, seeing no other way for their faith to survive, they made a conscious decision to leave the congregational model and find growth, fellowship, and mission beyond it.

While many will celebrate the discovery that the church of Jesus Christ is broader and more robust than our local institutions can contain, others find the news disturbing and prefer to reject or ignore the study. In a webinar with Dr. Packard shortly after the book was published, many of the chat messages to the moderator expressed displeasure that they were giving voice to this research. One denominational bookstore chain refused to carry the book, fearful of its influence on its congregations.

They either don't believe its conclusions or want to ignore them as a threat to their own future. Because they define the church institutionally they can cast aspersions on the faith of anyone who does not belong. That's why many have responded to declining attendance by doubling-down on obligation to keep people attending. Some religious leaders have a lot invested in marginalizing those who no longer participate in a local fellowship, lest others follow them out the door.

Interestingly, Dr. Packard is not encouraging people to leave their local congregations. In fact, he attends one and hopes that this study will help pastors to innovate ways to engage their most capable members so they won't feel the need to look elsewhere. Traditional congregations serve a valuable purpose where they teach people to live out their faith and where they incubate authentic community. It's just that there are not many who do that well anymore.

Twenty-five years ago, I would have been shocked at this research myself. As a pastor, I thought our program essential to faith and saw people outside of it as bitter lone rangers who were just angry that they couldn't get their way. One day, through the betrayal of a close friend, I found myself for the first time outside the congregation. Of course, I could have gone elsewhere, but found my heart hungering for a more authentic journey than any fellowship I'd been a part of was able to foster. And I soon discovered I was not alone.

That's why Dr. Packard's research did not come as a surprise to me. For the past two decades, I've been living among those who have found a vibrant life in Jesus as well as community outside of any religious institution. They are passionate, caring, committed disciples who want to see the kingdom of God grow in the world. They have been scorned, condemned, and maligned by those who reject their faith simply because they stopped attending Sunday services.

If you care about the future of the church in the Western world, you'll want to avail yourself of Packard and Hope's book. Whether you are one of the Dones, or concerned about people leaving your congregation, you'll at least want to understand why. I appreciate those who have found a local congregation in which to live out their spiritual journey and share community with others. There are good reasons, however, why that environment doesn't work for everyone.

My hope in writing this book is to help people not condemn those who see church differently than they do, but that we will come to celebrate all the ways that Jesus is inviting people to himself and recognize his church in the many ways she takes shape in the world.

CHAPTER 2

. . . .

IS CHURCH REFUGEES
A GAME CHANGER?

I had hoped it would be.

But, alas, the powers that lead our religious institutions wouldn't let it.

In *Church Refugees*, Dr. Josh Packard and Ashleigh Hope made a surprising and unexpected discovery. They identified a significant number of Christians who no longer attend church services and yet are thriving spiritually. To their surprise they discovered that most of them had not lost interest in their faith, faded out the back door, or preferred to watch football on Sundays. Instead they discovered them to be high-capacity Christians who were committed givers and deeply involved in leadership. They didn't leave quickly or easily, having spent years trying to encourage change or simply find a way to get along.

They eventually left because in all conscience they concluded that the way things were being done in their congregation threatened to compromise their faith. They sought community over judgment, mission over machinery, rich conversation over pat answers, and meaningful engagement with the world beyond moral prescriptions. While leaving was not easy as they suffered the judgments of former friends and colleagues, they soon discovered that there are plenty of resources for growth, meaningful connections with others on a faith journey, and ways to touch the world beyond the Sunday morning systems.

This book could have been a game changer for how we perceive the church and understand those who no longer find their Christian institutions the best or only way to express the reality of Jesus' kingdom. It had the potential to obliterate the myth that our local institutions are the only expressions of the church worthy of note. That's not what the authors had in mind, since they are both avid attenders themselves. They simply wanted to explore the phenomenon while seeking to help congregations understand why these people are leaving, and perhaps reconsider how to revitalize their institutions so they wouldn't feel the need to.

It is a compelling read that is hard to put down. The researchers mix their findings with firsthand stories from their respondents that will challenge whatever view you hold of the church. No doubt many will find it difficult to admit that passionate followers of Jesus are thriving outside our institutions, preferring the narrative that you can't be a true Christian if you are not connected to a local congregation. The hungers, however, are real, and if they won't be served by our existing congregations, people will look elsewhere. Obligation alone will not save these institutions.

For those who have already left, you'll find encouragement

that you're not alone in your desire for a more vibrant experience with God and his church and that it is possible to fulfill it in other ways. However, the terminology the authors use will make you cringe at times. Even the title, *Church Refugees*, is more than a little condescending to those who are no longer part of a traditional church. Calling them "The Dones" or the "De-churched" doesn't help either, and you'll find that language on almost every page. Keep in mind that the authors are sociologists and they are using those terms consistently with the terminology of their profession, where "church" is used to describe formal, religious institutions, not necessarily the bride of Christ as she appears in the world.

That's why those not engaged with a local institution are called "de-churched," though it does not dismiss the sincerity of their faith. Admittedly the term is awkward and one I wouldn't use, for the church Jesus is building is far bigger than what our institutions seek to contain. I've not been an active participant in an institutional church for over twenty years, but I don't consider myself a church refugee or that I am de-churched. I have never been more alive and engaged with the church Jesus is building in the world in so many expressions outside our traditional congregations. The church in Scripture was never a religious institution with weekend services and top-heavy bureaucracies. The church is the family Jesus is building in the earth and it cannot be contained or managed in any human organization. While it can take expression there, it also takes shape in many ways beyond it.

That's why I consider *Church Refugees* to be the most important church book written in this decade. Whether you like what their research shows or not, Packard and Hope have done us all a service by giving us an accurate picture of the religious landscape rather than relying on our biases or experiences. What we do with it will have great impact on our engagement with the church.

If you share the hunger of the Dones but still hold hope for our Christian institutions, it will help you be a voice for change so those hungers can be served instead of frustrated. If you've found it necessary to leave, you'll find great encouragement in knowing there are others finding opportunities for growth, deep fellowship, and mission beyond the programs of our congregations.

Hopefully it will help us all see the church as a bigger reality than our human conventions can contain, and affirm that what's most important is whether or not people are following Jesus, not which building they go to on Sunday morning, or even if they go to one at all.

Unfortunately, in the years that followed, the conversation did not materialize as broadly as I had hoped. Our Christian media serves the religious institutions as its market, and though many of them took a brief look at the book, they did not wrestle with the implications of it or invite a deeper conversation with those who have been alienated from religious institutions. Those with an institution-only mindset about the church seemed to circle the wagons and post a plethora of articles that propped up the age-old myth that church attendance is a requirement of the Gospel.

All the while, the exodus will continue until we recognize that the community of Christ's church cannot be built on obligation or institutional priorities. We may yet find the conversation that brings his church together beyond its various manifestations in the world.

My hope is that it would be sooner rather than later.

CHAPTER 3

. . . .

WHY ARE PEOPLE LEAVING?

What does it take for someone to leave a congregation of people they have loved and served alongside, often for decades? Why would they suddenly break away from close friends and lifetime traditions to wander into a lonely and uncertain future, only to be accused of being selfish, bitter, or rebellious by some of their closest friends and family?

Except that it usually isn't sudden at all. Though there came a day when they stopped attending, none of those I've met over the past twenty years left easily or suddenly. Most have wrestled with the decision for years in the face of some concern or unmet hunger. Initially they thought others around them would resonate with their passion, or be grateful if they identified a problem that needed attention. To their shock, they found their repeated attempts to discuss their concerns or hopes fell on unsympathetic ears.

Try as they might to bring positive changes, they only meet resistance and eventually disrespect and frustration. "That's not the way we do things around here." Many give up trying to convince others, but their hunger continues to grow until sitting in the congregation becomes increasingly painful. After years of struggle they finally feel they have no other choice but to follow their hunger instead of quietly going along. As much as they want to stay with people they care so much about, they find they can no longer participate in services that have become detrimental to their spiritual passions.

While the process is similar for most that I know, the reasons can be quite different. Recently I asked people on my Facebook page what it was that finally made it clear that they needed to leave their congregation. I got over a hundred responses from people that were consistent with the thousands of stories I have heard ove the last two decades.

» Forty-two percent said they were worn out by the machinery and the need to serve it. Some of that is burnout from having to do more than they had time or energy for, but for most it means that the cost it exacted wasn't worth the fruit it produced. Rarely does anyone say the congregation was all bad except in the most abusive cases. Mostly they say the demands of the congregation began to displace their passion for Jesus and that scared them.

» Twenty-three percent said they no longer respected the leadership because they were dishonest, autocratic, or manipulative. This didn't result from a bad confrontation or two, but a series of experiences that consistently eroded their trust and respect.

» Twenty percent said they simply hungered for more authentic relationships, feeling the ones they had were too superficial or governed by pat answers instead of people really getting to know them and wanting to walk alongside them in their joys and struggles.

» Twelve percent wanted more of Jesus and his life than their congregation offered. The focus seemed to be on things rather than helping people learn to experience the fullness of life in him.

» Three percent reported no dissatisfaction at all, but simply felt led by the Spirit to move on to a different stage of their journey.

Of course, my pool of respondents did not include those who gave up on God when they gave up on their church. Many do, seeing the failures of their institutions or its leaders as proof that God doesn't exist, or if he does, he at least doesn't care about them. It's a tragic legacy of our religious systems that do more to perpetuate programs than demonstrate Father's reality to those who seek after him.

But for every person who has left, be they pastor or parishioner, there are others who are thinking about it every time they sit through another service that doesn't address their deepest hungers. Many stay because of the relationships, others out of obligation no matter how painful it becomes. Actually, they are "done" too, attending in body only and with decreasing frequency, and it is only a matter of time before they stop as well.

Simply put, most of those who left did so because their spiritual passion could no longer be fulfilled where they were. So, what may look like someone just walked out one day isn't true. It is almost always a long, protracted process that even they resisted until they could do so no longer and still be true to their conscience.

The process is hard on everyone. In the first few months many of those who leave are racked with guilt and second-guess their decision frequently, especially if it is difficult to find others on the outside who share their hungers. And it's hard on those they leave behind, who feel rejected and concerned. Harsh words and judgments are too often exchanged as each side seeks to convince themselves they are doing what's right and need to convince the others for their own validation.

Those who have left are not your enemy. If they were your friends before, wouldn't they still be your friends now even if you are concerned for them? Wouldn't loving each other be vastly more important than how we gather or don't gather on a Sunday morning? Maybe if we were less threatened by their hunger we could celebrate their desire to find an environment more meaningful to their faith.

Certainly, some who leave find their way back when they can't find the community they are looking for. Most, however, after a year or two begin to find themselves connecting to others who share their hunger for more authentic and generous community in small groups or growing friendships, without the need or expense of sustaining the institutional machinery. They spend more time in conversations that nurture their faith and less time planning meetings and maintaining structures.

People who lose hope that the institutional model can provide a lifetime environment for community and growth may not be the death knell for the vitality of the church; maybe they are the hope that there's more than one way Jesus' church takes expression in the world.

CHAPTER 4

. . . .

FIVE FACTORS CONTRIBUTING TO THE DECLINE IN "CHURCH" ATTENDANCE

According to sociologist Josh Packard, thirty-one million people are no longer attending a local congregation but remain passionately engaged with their faith in Christ. That's the same number of people who attend services each weekend. What's more, seven million of those who attend will likely add to the number of those leaving in the near future.

What are we to make of all of this? Some pastors have suggested that those leaving are just being selfish at a time when the family needs them most. That's not true of the ones I've met over the last twenty years. They didn't leave out of selfishness, but in exasperation that their best attempts to inspire change in their congregation fell on deaf ears. They haven't given up on the church, but are looking for more authentic expressions of her.

So why are so many people leaving now? I see five cultural

factors that have converged in our time to contribute to this exodus:

The trend away from community.

Fifty years ago, most local churches were gathering places of a community that had been built over generations and acted as a large, extended family. The church growth movement of the '70s and '80s put a premium on size and with the advent of megachurches, real community was lost in the drive for bigger-is-better. Most people found themselves sitting in a room full of strangers. Many tried to address the need with various incarnations of home-group programs, but they failed largely because they were too heavily managed and focused more on the meeting than encouraging real friendships to grow. They didn't spawn community and most relationships were superficial at best.

The appeal to the casual Christian.

In the drive for increased size, much of this program was designed to appeal not to the passionate Jesus follower, whom leaders assumed would come anyway, but to those less-engaged who needed more entertainment than substance during their once-a-week attendance. When the professional sports teams realized their economic growth depended on attracting the casual fan, they substantively changed the nature of their sport to make sure they were entertained. It worked. Viewership skyrocketed, but for many hard-core fans, that ruined the game they'd fallen in love with. While that might work for football, it has not worked with the Gospel. The passionate followers of Jesus are leaving and many pastors are concerned that they are being left with those who only have a casual interest in spirituality.

The decline of cultural pressure.

It used to be true that to have credibility as a Christian in the local community, or to at least be available to that market, you needed a presence in a local fellowship. Those who didn't were looked down upon. That isn't true anymore and people have lots of options to fill their weekend. People no longer feel obligated by outward pressure and the stigma of not attending no longer exists outside the walls of a local fellowship.

The systematizing of spirituality that bypasses the heart in favor of the intellect.

Seminaries prepared academics to instruct the faithful, but left out the heart connection that enlivens spirituality. God is knowable in the inner life of a person, not just through a sermon, a text, or a Bible class. By not helping people connect more relationally with God they created a spiritual hunger in people that intellectual understanding alone couldn't satisfy. Instead of engaging their passion, they settled for obligation and guilt as motivations of faith and have left people worn out, frustrated, and empty.

The availability of alternative views.

It used to be that those who struggled with the program thought they were alone. That was easy to maintain as long as there were gatekeepers controlling the ideas people could engage. When distribution of material used to be expensive, it was impossible to publish literature that challenged the status quo since most publishers thought pastors' recommendations were critical to sales. Now anyone can publish a book, post articles on the Internet, or share a podcast with the world. People are finding out that they were not alone in their concerns about the impotence of the institutional program. They and many others desire a more vital spiritual life personally and a more engaging experience of community with others.

* * * * * *

That these factors would converge at this time in religious history may point to something far larger than selfish people leaving to pursue their own interests. This exodus may in fact be a move of the Spirit to revitalize Jesus' church for the days to come. People are not abandoning the church, only those structures that no longer make room for her to thrive in their midst.

So, while some look at thirty-one million people walking away as cause for alarm, I find it encouraging. People are taking their faith seriously and if the congregation they attend isn't expressing that journey, they are willing at great personal risk to look elsewhere, not just to another institution but to more relational ways to engage God and others. They are finding a more authentic spirituality that is allowing them to love more freely in the world.

This is an exciting time in church history. We are finding out what expressions the church can take when people deeply engaged with God find ways to connect and collaborate in the world without the rigors of institutionalism. I am hopeful that they will better express the nature of God in the world than our tired institutions are currently doing. This is a great time to be alive.

. . . .

CHAPTER 5

I'M LOOKING FOR THIRTY-FIVE MILLION PEOPLE

Nothing breaks my heart more than meeting someone who invested years of their life in religious service and for some reason never discovered how real God is and how deeply he loves them.

According to *Church Refugees*, thirty-five million Americans left their religious institution and abandoned their belief in God at the same time. I'm fine with them leaving. Religious institutions can often impede our spiritual growth rather than encourage it. But my heart breaks for those who left not knowing a God worth loving. That means despite all the meetings they attended, prayers they offered, and good deeds they did, they never came face to face with the most endearing Presence in the universe. They never recognized his voice wooing them, or recognized his hand at work in their life. In the end, the church and its activities were the god they knew, and somehow they missed the real one.

Sadly, I understand why they would miss him. Insecure

religious leaders who try to rule with an iron fist or simply don't know him themselves, and legalistic religious traditions that substitute rules and rituals for helping connect people to the transcendent God, can be barriers to the very faith people want to explore. Some say you can't have God without religion; it's a package deal. If you want to be one of his you have to jump through the time-established hoops to prove your sincerity.

But those who say so are usually trying to build or sustain an institution for their own purposes. What they teach isn't true. While some congregations can help people discover God's reality, many others are a deterrent. Jesus didn't start an institution, or a religion, for that matter. He came to reveal to us what it would be like to live in his Father's reality—how his love would change us and how our loving others in the world would let his kingdom unfold around us.

That's why the Apostle Paul didn't try to win people with "wise and persuasive words," because he didn't want people's faith to "rest on human wisdom, but on God's power." If your spiritual passion was only based on following someone else's teachings it wasn't going to last anyway; it was always going to fail you.

So, I'm looking for you. If I could sit down to lunch with any of these thirty-five million people, this is what I would want you to know:

> » Religious obligation is a conformity-based system that operates by fear and manipulation and that's why it could not promote the love of God growing in your heart. But don't give up. Look elsewhere, mostly with someone who already knows him. Walking with God as he really is, is the greatest adventure life offers.

» Separate the failures of religion and religious leaders from the reality of God. Jesus did. The Pharisees had God wrong, which is why they didn't understand his love for sinners, or his refusal to conform to their traditions. It is why they killed him.

» Consider the possibility that you were given a disfigured view of God, especially if you see him as an angry tyrant wanting to rule the world through terror. He is actually a gracious Father who loves you more than anyone else on this planet ever has or ever will.

» Recognize where God is already reaching out to you. That voice inside your head that invites you away from the anxieties of this life is his drawing you to himself. Those transcendent moments when you knew you were not alone in the universe and that Someone endearing holds you and this world in his hands, were his doing to nudge you toward the relationship he desires with you.

» God was not the cause behind the latest natural disaster, your best friend dying, your financial difficulties, or your disappointments in life. He wasn't punishing you or them for their failures to see him or follow him. This world is out of sync with its Creator and the effects of that touch us all with sin, sickness, and pain. God is not the cause of those problems. He's the rescuer in the story, inviting us away from the mayhem and into the knowing of him.

» Ask him to reveal himself to you and to send you someone who can help you learn to follow him.

All that Jesus said was true. There is a place for you to be at home in God, and for God to be at home in you. Don't give up that pursuit just because an institution failed you. Just ask God, "If you are real, would you show yourself to me?"

Do it.

He will.

CHAPTER 6

. . . .

YOUR ATTENDANCE IS NOT REQUIRED

I'm increasingly concerned that Christianity in our day is devolving into a human religion loosely based on the teachings of Jesus, while missing the point of them all.

Every week I get links to blogs and articles of various pastors giving the five, eight, or twelve reasons everyone needs to attend a local church each week. To prove their point, however, they have to make absurd statements that have no grounding in the life or character of Jesus. These conclusions are not just misguided, but actually destructive to people who want to grow in his life and joy.

This is not a personal judgment against them. I'm sure many of them are fine people, only trying to do what they feel called to do. I also appreciate that this is a scary time for them as so-called church attendance is on the decline. The idea that someone can actually grow in their relationship with God, experience the wonder of Jesus' church as she takes shape in the world, and be involved in his mission to the lost without being part of *their* congregation has to be a scary concern, especially if your job depends on it. Many don't even want to acknowledge it is even possible, so they double down on the language of obligation and accountability. In doing so, however, they twist the Gospel so that it is no longer recognizable, and all that's left is for people to obey what they are told by leadership whose success and livelihood depend on that obedience.

There are many good reasons to gather regularly with other believers and share the journey of faith. It's just that all those gatherings are not going on in Sunday morning services shackled by the bureaucracy of a religious system, which often does more to stifle spiritual growth than stimulate it. Many have found more engaging ways to share the life of the church beyond the walls of traditional congregations, and telling them they must attend a normal service falls on deaf ears once they've discovered that it isn't true.

So, if they hope guilt and obligation will win these people back or scare the ones they have into remaining, they are not only fighting a losing battle but disfiguring God and distorting the Gospel to do it. The life of the church is not found in obligation but in the joy of affection and transformation. Trying to discount the salvation of those who leave in hopes of reining back in the faithful will continue to backfire.

Here's an example of that kind of reasoning. This is by Nathan Rose, a Missouri pastor in the Southern Baptist denomination who says that skipping "church" meetings is dangerous to your health. He gives five reasons why in a recent article he wrote called "Five Spiritual Dangers of Skipping Church":

1. "You will miss out on God's primary design for your spiritual growth and well-being." What in the ministry of Jesus leads him to the conclusion that God's primary means to grow to spiritual maturity is to attend a church service weekly, when he never conducted one himself, never taught his disciples how to do so, and assigned the task for our growth to the Holy Spirit who would dwell in us and guide us to all truth? When the Samaritan woman asked Jesus where she should worship, he made it clear that location is not the issue. What matters is that we do so in spirit and in truth. Living in the Father's affection and responding to his Spirit within us is God's primary design for our growth and well-being, not sitting in a pew on Sunday morning.

2. "You disobey God." As many do, Rose pulls out Hebrews 10:24-25, saying that the counsel "not to neglect to meet together" is a command that can only be fulfilled in a weekly church service. It's dishonest on the face of it. This is the only Scripture pastors have to seek to compel "church attendance" and it is misused at that. This passage wasn't written to believers skipping out on church services, but to people under persecution who were wondering if avoiding association with each other would make it more difficult for the authorities to find them. The writer is telling them they have more to gain by the encouragement they have from each other than going it alone. Most Sunday services don't even allow

people to encourage each other, since the focus is on the platform. Hebrews 10 is not talking about attending a meeting; it is about staying connected to others and treasuring their lives and encouragement. In all honesty, many of today's institutions do more to inhibit that connection than encourage it.

3. "You make a statement to the world that God is not worthy of worship..., which is the attitude and conduct of unbelievers, not God's people." So if you don't come to "worship" you are no longer one of God's people. The judgment here is frightful. Worship is not a song service or a sermon, but a life lived in God's reality and his affection. How we see him and how we love and respect others either brings glory to him or disfigures him. Sitting in a pew on Sunday morning is not a statement of how important worship is to you unless that's the only way you understand worship, and then you are spiritually impoverished the rest of the week. Our lives worship him whether we're on the job, enjoying his creation, or serving someone in need.

4. "You can't minister to anyone." Really? All the ministry that God wants to do in the world can only happen under a steeple on Sunday morning? That thought would be hilarious if its assumptions weren't so tragic. Jesus never consigned his ministry in a "service," but on the street where he encountered people. Real service is not sitting in a pew so others can hear you sing and you can show support for the

pastor. Ministry is about loving and helping people you know or come across as you go through life. They can be in your neighborhood, at work, in school, or across the world.

5. "You skip out on a foretaste of heaven." If Sunday morning services were really a foretaste of heaven, no one would want to miss them and you wouldn't have to obligate them to be there. In many cases it's just a repeated formula often laced with guilt and condemnation, as was this entire piece written by Rose.

What bothers me most is not that they want people to come to "their church," but that they see obligation as the reason. They make the same mistake the Galatians made. By turning the promise of God into an obligation they distort the gospel, twisting the joy of an invitation into God's life into demands and threats. It has the underlying psychology of "misery loves company." We are not here because we enjoy it and God works in us, but because God says we have to. Please! The kingdom is the pearl of great price, not the castor oil of spiritual health.

Paul, the apostle, encourages us to live in freedom and let "no one" defraud us by telling us where we should go, what we should eat, or what we should wear. People who try to tell you what you should do, rather than equipping you to live fully and freely in Jesus, have lost connection with the Head.

I honestly feel sorry for those who can't see the reality of Christ's church beyond their own congregation or the congregational model itself. They would perhaps do better to take an honest look at why people who were committed members of their congregation found it necessary to leave. Badgering them with accusations and demands will never fulfill the work of the kingdom.

Maybe it is time for them to ask just how accurately their institution reflects God's nature and reality. Those who honestly seek to help people live in the reality of Jesus' freedom and transformation need not be threatened that Jesus is also working outside their borders.

In fact, if they put his kingdom first, they will rejoice that he does.

CHAPTER 7

· · · · · · · · · · · · ·

HOW MUCH DID PAUL GET IT WRONG?

The sunshine was brilliant as we gathered in a field along the English coast with some of our friends from throughout Europe. I sat down next to Dave, a former South African now residing in Ireland. As we got reacquainted he asked with just a touch of mischief in his voice, "Do you want to know what I've been thinking about these days?"

Of course, I did! I know Dave can be playful, but he is a serious follower of Jesus and a provocative thinker.

He leaned over and in a surreptitious whisper said, "I've been wondering just how much Paul got it wrong."

I just shook my head chuckling, wondering where this would lead. It was a loaded question to be sure, though our ensuing conversation helped clarify that he was less focused on what Paul got wrong as he was how wrongly we interpret Paul. We read his letters as if he wrote them last week to the denominations and megachurches of the twenty-first century. The early believers he was writing to, however, were not organized into the same large institutions we have today, with their complex political and economic structures.

We mistakenly assume that when Paul wrote about worship he was referring to the songs and prayers we use to start a service, teaching as a lecture to a room of passive listeners, that elders were the business leaders who made financial decisions for the corporation, or that pastors were pastor-preneurs carving out a niche in the religious market for their own income.

We forget that the early believers didn't do anything that resembled the way most congregations meet today, and when we co-opt the same terminology to justify our structures, we get Paul entirely wrong. For the most part, the new believers comprised informal networks of those who gathered around specific households. While those in Corinth gathered on the first day of the week, we don't know that everyone else did. Paul even wrote to the Romans that some might consider a specific day special and others all the same and there was freedom in Christ for that.

But we are certain those believers didn't sit in pews watching a production on stage, nor that they allowed a single person to dominate the life of the congregation. When that happened in Ephesus, John called out Diotrephes as evil (3 John 9-11) for lording it over the others. At the same time he affirms Demetrius for the quality of his life. Do we really imagine that these two were pitted against each other in a board meeting for control of the congregation? They were not that centralized until later, as human leaders wanted the same kind of control over the faithful that Diotrephes held.

No, I don't think Paul got it wrong. I appreciate everything he wrote and the invitation he gave to live in a vibrant relationship with Jesus, rather than get sucked into living by law, or in submitted compliance to so-called leaders who want people to follow them instead of following Christ. Many mistakenly think that Paul's writings are our guide for right faith and practice, completely ignoring Jesus' words that he would send us his Spirit and that *he* would guide us into all truth. Jesus never even mentioned that a collection of writings would one day come together to make following his Spirit obsolete. Even Paul would abhor much of how we apply his writings today. He wrote to encourage people to follow the Spirit rather than to craft a New Testament code of ethics or set up a hierarchy of leadership.

I embrace the Bible as a God-inspired collection of writings to give us the truth about God and how he revealed himself in the world, but it is designed to equip us to live a life in the Spirit, not to replace him or his touch in our lives. You can tell when someone is interpreting Paul with the blinders of their religious institutions when they use his quotes to justify their religious systems. Their conclusions will reflect far more the management styles of the world than they do the vibrant community of the new creation. While Paul uses similar words as pastor and elder, what he means by them is markedly different than how we use them today. He was talking about older brothers and sisters with character who can discern between true and false living while encouraging younger believers to a more genuine faith, not about those with a seminary pedigree and the charisma to draw a crowd.

One of the glaring differences when you read Paul and look at how most people think of church today, is how it has moved from being a "we" to being an "it." It lost its vitality as a community of the redeemed sharing their joy and gifts, and became an institution that seeks control over Christ's followers.

I appeared on a radio discussion not long ago on the topic, "Is Church Attendance Mandatory?" I was asked to explain why so many people are leaving traditional Christian institutions and whether or not they could still be considered followers of Christ. The discussion was amiable enough but as my host signed off, she used a well-known quote from Cyprian, the Bishop of Carthage in the middle of the third century. "He can no longer have God for his Father who has not the church for his mother." Her conclusion was clear: you cannot be a follower of Christ if you're outside a local, sanctioned institution. I would love to see how Paul would respond to that!

The quote is silly on the face of it. If we as God's children comprise the church, then how can we be our own mother? We are siblings with God as Father and Christ our Head. As far as I know, Cyprian's statement is one of the first that redefined the church from a "we" to an "it." And this "it" is a mother demanding our obedience and conformity. In doing so the early bishops quite intentionally exalted themselves above the family and inserted themselves as mediators between Jesus and his followers. You follow him by following "it."

Less than 250 years after Christ died and Paul wrote his letters, the freedom of the new creation had been fully crushed by the institution that calls itself "church." And it is even more distressing that a Protestant in our day would appeal to such a quote, since Cyprian's context was that of the authority of what became the Catholic Church specifically. My host was already out of compliance to the mandatory allegiance to which she referred. The irony was perhaps lost to her since Protestants claim the same fidelity to their systems that the early bishops demanded of theirs.

Isn't this when things went horribly wrong? People were no longer invited to follow Christ; they had their bishop to follow or rituals to observe, mostly based on someone's interpretations of Paul's writings. I've always wondered how one can know God as Father and end up so far off course. And why would they be so convinced of it that they would damn any who disagree with them? If you don't attend our meetings, participate in our rituals, join our membership, or sign our covenant, you are excluded from Christ and his salvation.

And I do understand the concerns today. Many who claim to follow Jesus are only following their own self-interest and stumble off into error. It's easy to think that the institutional control of "more mature" brothers and sisters would fix that problem. But it doesn't; it only shifts the problem. It stagnates the spiritual growth of more sincere people by taking their eyes off of Jesus. When the size of any institution grows, it easily seduces those who lead it to serve their own self-interest, especially where income and ego are involved.

The only way to guarantee the future of a corporation is to make people dependent on it by making it mandatory for salvation. I remember the things I used to defend when my income directly benefited from my theology. It obscures our thinking more than we know. But to double-down on the obligation card is to ignore the reality of the Incarnation, the nature of the new creation, and the identity of his church growing in the world. Jesus came to be with us, not just while he was in the flesh, but now by the power of the Spirit.

If whatever we call "church" is not as engaging as Jesus was on the planet, then maybe we're not talking about *his* church. It certainly wasn't what Paul was describing, nor the reality he wrote about. Whether we belong to Jesus or not is demonstrated not by our attendance at a weekly meeting, but by his character taking shape in us and how we love those around us.

Paul said this was a freedom worth fighting for. He warned about people "cutting in" on them with rules and obligations, of being robbed of their freedom, and told them not to "let anyone tell you what you should do..." He made no exceptions for bishops or pastors. He wanted people following Christ as he made himself known, not substituting anyone or anything for that vibrancy of life in him.

The life of the church will never be found in accountability to people or systems, but in the love of Christ taking root in our lives. For that it needs a growing number of people who take following Christ seriously and themselves less so. It is worth risking the anger and judgment of those who seek to steal that freedom, and instead learn how to recognize his work in you. You follow Jesus by actually following Jesus, not by living up to the expectations of those who set themselves up as leaders.

That is such a foreign concept to people that when many leave a congregation, they feel lost for a time. The question I get most often from them is, "Now, what should I do?" The worst indictment of the failure of our institutions is that people no longer have any idea how to follow Christ without rituals and guidelines from the outside. Instead of being equipped to follow Jesus, they were lulled to spiritual passivity by a well-planned program. This, more than anything, accounts for the emptiness people feel and why they go look for something else. But even then, they will naturally seek a set of activities to sustain them.

The response I give them is, "Follow him!" It's the best counsel ever! Even if they don't know how to yet, they are now going to get to learn. The most important questions become not what should I do, but how do I get to know him? What is he revealing in my life? How is his love shaping me to live more freely in the world? Who is he asking me to walk alongside now, both those who help me and those I can help?

Some people find connection in other established groups. If they do, I encourage them to go for the relationships, not the program. Any structure is helpful only to the degree that it equips people to live in the Spirit and to share community. When it subverts either mission, ignore it. Others will find connection more informally with friends, neighbors, and coworkers who share their journey of faith together in an ongoing conversation.

Our faith was meant to be an adventure of waking up in him each day and asking him to lead us. As he nudges your heart to connect with someone or do something in the world, follow him. Don't overly spiritualize it. If it feels right in your heart and it is loving to do, give it a try. See if it bears the fruit of his kingdom. If not, consider what else he might have before you. As you follow those nudges, love freely the people who cross your path, and follow up on any leads toward others who might be hungering for more of a family connection, it will eventually become clear how Father is knitting you into his family.

In that adventure, Paul's writings become so much more powerful. You'll begin to see that worship is not about singing songs, but living our lives in Father's reality. As we let him live his life through us, gratitude will rise in our hearts and in the lives of others we touch. We'll discover that ninety percent of teaching happens in a conversation where someone asks a question or makes an observation that causes lights to go on inside and draws others closer to Jesus. Elders are seasoned saints whose life and character back up the theology they espouse, and they freely offer their time to help others learn to live inside the life and freedom of Jesus.

So, when you read Paul, check your biases. Is he referring to the church as a collection of hundreds of thousands of institutions who often have very little to do with each other, or is he talking about a family that is learning to love each other the way Jesus loves them? When he talks about the church of Jesus Christ as the bride being prepared for his Son, don't be tempted to think that he's referring to an institution with a cute contemporary name and a mandatory meeting designed to keep people on the straight and narrow. Paul would have never seen it that way.

Instead he would be seeing a vibrant community of men and women faithfully following Jesus as they connected locally, sharing that journey with endearing friendships.

CHAPTER 8

. . . .

DO YOU NEED COVERING?

Perhaps no teaching has been used more to subjugate the will of one human to another than that of spiritual covering. Under the guise of spiritual authority, people are actually instructed to obey a religious leader, even at the cost of not following Jesus himself.

I don't hear much talk of it stateside anymore, though I know it's here, but it came up often in a recent trip through South Africa. Spiritual covering is the idea that as a believer you need something or someone above you to protect you from deception and error. Some traditions teach that your local pastor or congregation is your covering. As long as you follow their teachings and submit critical decisions to them, they will keep you from slipping off the narrow way. Others claim they are covered by a denomination or denominational executive, or even the Pope himself.

It assumes God only works through hierarchical leadership

structures and if you don't follow them, you are not following Christ. If you have a covering, God will protect and bless you. If you do not, you are in rebellion and not only can the enemy deceive you, but also God will not care for you.

Those who teach this false doctrine use it to exploit people and demand their unquestioned obedience. Those who believe it are paralyzed by fear, especially when the Spirit inside is trying to warn them away from leaders who are exploiting them. It confuses people when God reveals in them things that run counter to the desires of their leaders. In those moments, they will find it easier to believe they must be wrong, and defer to the alleged anointing, education, or charisma of the leader. It's no wonder we have so many weak and confused Christians who are dependent on someone else to tell them what to believe or do.

It's amazing how much traction this doctrine has gained over the centuries, especially when it has absolutely no biblical support! Chalk that up to the fact that those teaching it are beneficiaries of it, whether to sate their ego or garner their income. Nothing in Scripture is written that tells us we are safer following a human leader than we are following the Spirit Jesus gave us. On the contrary, much is written warning us against it.

The only place in Scripture where covering is mentioned is Adam and Eve using fig leaves after the fall. Their shame sought a covering to hide from God and each other. So why does their first reaction to sin become our model for safety, especially when it's God they were hiding from? And that's exactly what happens under covering theology. It puts someone or something between you and God to protect you from him, and to surrender your allegiance to another flawed human being. Not surprisingly, it also fragments the body of Christ as we divide up into separate fiefdoms of covering.

The only other Scripture I've heard quoted in the defense of covering is Hebrews 13:17: "Obey your leaders and submit to their authority. They keep watch over you as men who must give an account." The first part of this verse is intentionally translated to overhype ecclesiastical authority. The early followers didn't have institutional structures or those managing them that people had to submit to unquestioningly. They had relationships with more mature followers, and this verse encouraged them to yield to their wisdom as they learned to follow God themselves. These leaders didn't tell people what to do, but taught them to engage God and to follow him.

The second part of this verse is often twisted to teach that believers are accountable to human leaders, when the clear meaning of the verse is that the leaders are accountable to God for what they teach and how they treat his people. Jesus never intended that those who lead in his kingdom would get between him and his people. The glory of the new covenant is that "all will know him, from the least to the greatest," and that they will be able to follow him because he will write his ways on their hearts and minds (Hebrews 8). True leaders equip people to know Christ and to follow him, not get people to follow them instead.

In *Finding Church*, I wrote of a friend from Australia who drew a great distinction between elders in the first-century church and what elders became in the second generation. Ignatius, a disciple of John the apostle, helped make that twist. Prior to Ignatius, elders were seen as guardians of a gift— "Christ in you, the hope of glory." Every believer was a temple in which Christ dwelled, and elders guarded that gift from anyone trying to subjugate his followers to their own desires or vision. But as the early believers began to form hierarchical pyramids of authority, Ignatius demanded loyalty to leaders as guardians of right faith and practice. Thus, in one generation, leadership had changed from those who equip others to follow the Spirit within, to those who would conform them to rules and doctrine from without. Instead of serving people's spiritual journeys, they became policemen to compel people to do what they thought best.

This covering theology may well have been one of those "doctrines of demons" Paul warned us to reject. For under the guise of protecting people from Satan's deception, they take them captive to their own will or wisdom. People are taught to trust some other person's "anointing" or academic training. But it simply doesn't work. I've never met a pastor or other leader who got caught in a sexual affair or misusing ministry funds who wasn't under a designated covering of some sort.

Wasn't it Lucifer's goal in the garden to separate the first humans from God, getting them to trust their own ways instead of his and cover up in their shame? Wasn't this what Israel expressed when they ran from God's presence, encouraging Moses to listen for them, promising they would obey him instead? And wasn't this why Samuel warned Israel that their desire for a king was a rejection of God and would backfire on them in ways they couldn't imagine?

We have a long history of wanting to put someone or something between God and us in the misguided fear that God can't lead us personally. And didn't those choices always inure them to the dangers of handing over power and control to human leaders? To the detriment of humanity, their designated leaders would end up serving their own interests, rather than God's. It gives away responsibility for what's true to someone who is usually vested in our response to it. Some of the dearest people I know get their agenda and God's confused quite easily, and all the more so when their livelihood depends on it.

The Incarnation of Jesus invited each of us inside a relationship with him where he would be our shepherd. He said that his sheep would know his voice and that he will lead them into safe pasture so they would never need to be afraid again. The work of Jesus puts our trust in him, not religious leaders. Because he conquered sin and shame on the cross, we each have the opportunity to know him, not trust someone else to tell us what he's like. Any need for a covering was removed as we are given full and free access to God.

Can you imagine what would have happened if Jesus would have submitted to the "spiritual covering" of his day? The Pharisees would have silenced him and separated him from the very people he came to rescue. Unfortunately, the religious leaders of his day were among those who had most lost touch with God and his nature.

That's why Jesus didn't tell us he would send us a book to guide us, a religious structure to protect us, or spiritual leaders to control us. He said he would leave us with his Spirit who "would guide us into all truth." The reality of the New Testament community is that God lives in us all by the Spirit and thus has access to every heart and mind, and that those who know him would recognize that voice and follow him.

Though Paul told Timothy to appoint elders in Ephesus who could encourage people with sound doctrine, he did not intend for those elders to supplant Jesus or to infringe on his relationship with them. When they did, John wrote to Ephesus again many years later to let them know that the elders had become the problem, demanding allegiance to them over their obedience to Christ. He had to remind them that they each had an anointing from the Holy One so they could discern between what's true and what's not.

So, no, you do not need a covering to protect you spiritually. In fact, it will have the opposite effect if it convinces you that you cannot trust his Spirit within you to be your protection and guide. Does that mean, then, you're on your own and if a bit theologically naïve, you are at risk? If the Holy Spirit dwells in you, how could you be? He is able to keep you safe in the arms of the Father against any lie that would deceive you, whether it comes from the evil one or from the best-intentioned religious leader.

Haven't you heard a teacher say something that had all the biblical proof texts one could want, but left you restless inside, questioning whether something was amiss even if you couldn't identify it? Like a teaching on spiritual covering perhaps? That's his Spirit helping you discern what's true and what's false. When religious leaders teach you to trust them instead of the Spirit's compass within you, you'll get very confused as to how Jesus wants to lead you. Your allegiance belongs only to him, not to people or organizations who claim to speak for him.

But won't that lead to chaos and error when everyone does what is right in their own eyes? To the degree that people follow self instead of Jesus, it will. We all know people who claim to be led by the Spirit who do horribly self-serving and destructive things in his name. We might think it helpful if more mature brothers or sisters could rein that in with command authority, but Scripture gives no place for that to happen and history gives us no example where that authority was not soon corrupted to take people's eyes off of Jesus.

Jesus warned his disciples that they would not "lord over" others as demonstrated in the worldly structures around them (Mark 10:42-45). His leaders would be servants, not commanders. They help people come to know Christ and teach them how to follow him. History teaches us that whenever humans draw his authority to themselves, they will almost always end up using it in self-serving ways. They will make decisions for the good of the institution that employs them rather than the individual they were called to serve.

So how do we respond to spiritual authority? It is helpful to separate institutional authority from spiritual authority. They are not the same thing. If you are part of an institutional system, then yield to its way of keeping order or you'll only be a destructive source of division and chaos. When you can no longer follow along or feel it is compromising your own life with God, then you need to leave and see what else he has for you. Just because someone has authority in a system, that does not mean they have authority from God.

God's authority comes through the power of an indestructible life—the integrity and the authenticity demonstrated in how they live. They are not playing a role, but have simply learned to live in growing trust of God's love and can encourage others to do the same. Authority doesn't come from a vocation, academic training, or a place on the flow chart. They are people you respect not only for their insight and wisdom, but also for the tenderness and compassion with which they treat people. They do not marshal people to build their own kingdom, but build up others so they can follow Christ with greater freedom and joy.

When you are near someone at rest in God's goodness, though their insight may challenge you, you'll find them the safest people to be around in your struggles, failures, or questions. Give their words weight, but resist the urge to grow dependent on them instead of letting them help you learn to listen to God's Spirit in you.

No person is meant to be a covering between you and God. Anyone who seeks to tell you what to do on God's behalf proves by doing so that they are not acting in his authority. True leaders will speak the truth as they see it in love and entrust it to the Spirit and your conscience to convince you of what's true. They don't exploit people or demand their loyalty. They simply serve you, as Jesus grows bigger in your heart.

I know that some who read this will fear that people following Jesus without a human "covering" will become arrogant and independent, but I don't find that to be true. This is a family after all, not a free-for-all. They realize that Truth exists apart from their own preferences or best wisdom. Anyone seeking to follow Jesus, as he makes himself known within them, will soon realize that they navigate in uncertain space. As Paul says, we all see through a darkened mirror as we seek to discern his ways.

Perhaps that's why we want the security of the pseudo-confidence of anyone who claims to know it all or some doctrinal structure to protect us. But they are only an illusion. No one hears God perfectly, interprets Scripture with complete accuracy, or knows your heart like God does, which always makes me suspicious of those who proclaim certainty and speak as if their words are proclamations straight from God.

So where is our safety net, if there is no spiritual covering? Why, it is in him, of course! God the Father watches over you, Jesus walks with you, and his Spirit dwells in you. Having any other spiritual covering is an act of distrust in his ability to care for you. If we are wanting to follow his ways, he will let our hearts resonate with those things that are true and make us restless in those things that are false. In time, circumstances, and whether or not we are finding his fullness within, will help us learn where we are listening to him and where we are dressing up our own desires in God-language. If it doesn't become evident to us, it will become evident to those around us.

That's why learning to listen to him incubates a spirit of humility and openness. Those growing in Christ do not become independent or anarchist. Learning to follow Jesus is a lifelong journey, separating his desires and his way of working from our own. As we do, we will find ourselves able to see more clearly the difference between what is true and what is false.

Always look for what his Spirit is revealing to you to be consistent with the character of Scripture. Always treat most suspiciously those leadings that perfectly dovetail with your own desires and whims. God's ways are higher than ours, and his insights will challenge our conventional and preferred thoughts to lead us more deeply into his reality. Truth will almost always challenge us before our surrendering to it will set us free.

Anyone who willingly walks alone on this journey, and without the wisdom and counsel of others, is a fool. Find some other men and women you can share with and let their thoughts and insights help you discern how the Spirit is leading you, or whether you're just reacting to last night's pizza. Your friends won't always get it right, but they will help you find your blind spots. Be most careful when they are trying to talk you out of a difficult obedience, and most open when they help you see how pride or dishonesty is slipping in as our flesh tries to masquerade as his Spirit.

And in the big-ticket items of theology or direction, find others who are a bit further down the track than you. There are elders, teachers, prophets, and apostles who are gifts to help us know God better and learn his ways. Just know that the real ones don't carry the title on their business cards and are not building an institution in their name. At almost every stage where God has shifted my thinking, he put me alongside some older men and women who could encourage his work in me and provide warnings when I was being sidetracked. Those who are wise, gently honest, and without the need to control your response are great gifts. We need more of these genuine elders scattered in the body of Christ who are courageous enough to walk alongside others and encourage their growth without controlling them.

We also have opportunity to think alongside men and women who have lived before us by the writings they've left that have endured the test of time. Interact with their thoughts and see how they might apply to your own journey, especially those who have endured and thrived in their faith through dark and desperate times.

In these days of disintegrating institutions, Jesus is calling the church back to himself. As long as you are cowering beneath any kind of human-contrived covering, you'll ignore him in deference to them. He has made a way for you to be deeply connected to him, and he is more certain than any covering humanity can devise. Put your trust in him and look to follow him each day as best you see him.

I've heard some people, when asked what spiritual covering they are under, will respond that Jesus is the only covering they need. I get what they mean by that, but perhaps it is better said that Jesus came to do away with any need for covering at all. Now with unveiled faces we can behold him, and in doing so be transformed by him.

There's no good reason for anyone else to stand in the way of that.

CHAPTER 9

. . . .

SEVEN MARKERS TO HELP YOU WHEN YOU'RE DONE

A "Thrival" Guide for Those Who Find Themselves Outside of Conventional Congregations

People are leaving the local church in droves. Many do so while questioning whether God even exists, but many others continue to passionately follow Jesus, convinced that the institution they belonged to was at odds with the spiritual passion growing in their heart. They may not have even understood why, but something inside continued to draw them toward a more authentic relationship with Jesus and a freer environment to share his life and love with others.

Many who have given up on the traditional congregation were once leaders, volunteers, and major contributors. They grew weary of the programs and expectations that neither encouraged their journey nor cultivated the kind of community they sought. Leaving is never easy, and most do it only when other options are exhausted.

Finding yourself outside the congregational model can be incredibly disorienting for a season. Family and former friends question your faith or make you feel guilty with accusations of bitterness or selfishness. All the markers you used to gauge your spiritual health no longer make sense. Some question their own sanity, and even more so as they are increasingly isolated from the only friends they've ever had.

If you've left your congregation for similar reasons, what do you do now? As I've watched people go through this transition, the ones who navigate it most freely begin to embrace a different set of realities. These realities not only allow them to survive outside a local congregation, but actually help them to thrive in learning to follow him, in sharing fellowship with others, and in being part of God's purpose in the world.

First, take your time.

You've been invited on an amazing journey that will take years to sort out. Many people rush to join another congregation or start their own house group to fill the void, but only end up recreating what they had left. Resist the urge to find another group right away or to create one. This is a season to draw closer to God and let him fill the void. There will be time for more connections later when it's not a response to a driven need, but rather a freedom to embrace the gift of community that God wants to give you.

Second, don't force your journey on others.

You don't have to tell people, "I've left the church," or judge as less spiritual those who still go. This isn't about judging others or making outlandish conclusions about the future you can't begin to sort out yet. Simply follow Jesus, however he leads you, and be gently honest with those who ask you why you're not doing the things you used to.

Remember, you're the one who changed here; they are just

doing the things you've always done, with many convinced they are obligated to do so. They will be threatened by the change you're making, and you can help disarm that by letting them have their own journey. Don't try to change them, or to fix them. If they are in a place that diminishes their spiritual passion, you can't persuade them until the Spirit awakens the same hunger in them.

Third, lose your need to be validated by others.

Religion works by establishing a set of expectations, rewarding those who conform and punishing those who do not, usually by what other people think of you. When they question your decisions, it will be natural for you to get defensive and try to convince others how right you are. Doing so, however, will only harden them and destroy your friendships. You'll discover that the greatest freedom in this journey is to let Jesus break that cycle so that you can find your identity in his love for you alone. Slowly you'll find what God thinks of you, and your journey is far more important than what others think.

Trust that God will bring about the conversations you need, and even things to read, that will confirm that you are following him and not your own desires. Be gracious to all and let his affirmation of your life and experience be all the validation you need. Then you'll be free from the tyranny of other people's opinions of you.

Fourth, learn the beauty and rhythms of love.

Following ritual and rules that others demand of you is still following law, even if we call them "New Testament principles." God doesn't transform us through obligation or meeting the expectations of others. The reason why many of us grew frustrated in religious settings is because they made promises they couldn't fulfill. The harder we tried, the emptier we felt. God has been inviting you to live in a new creation where his love transforms us in the deepest part of our soul.

Over this season you'll learn to see through the manipulation of obligation, accountability, guilt, and fear and into a different rhythm that will allow you to live more at rest, aware of others, and free from the corrupting influences of this age. Instead of doing what others think you should do, you'll be freer to discern his work in you, and you'll find yourself embracing his realities of grace, forgiveness, freedom, and generosity.

It all begins as you ask him to show you how deeply loved by God you are, and then let him show you. This is the trailhead that will lead you to greater freedom and fullness.

Fifth, watch your trust in him grow.

Many are surprised to discover how much of their religious life was driven by fear—of God punishing them, of going astray, of what others will think, of missing out, or of failure. As you are more in touch with his love and delight in you, even when you're struggling or doubting, you'll find that your trust in his goodness will begin to grow. You'll realize he's for you, not against you, and that your own efforts were never going to produce his life in you. Now you'll discover the joy of cooperating with his work in you, and you'll find yourself more relaxed, more aware of his nudges and insight, and less inclined toward destructive and hurtful actions. When Paul talked about the righteousness that comes from faith, this is what he was talking about. Where we trust him, we won't try to save ourselves or force our way. Now we can know what it is to be content in him, whatever life brings to us, because he is walking with us through it.

Sixth, cultivate friendships with others.

God's love working in you will free you to love each person God puts in front of you. Take an interest in them, whether they already know God or not, and watch as they begin to open up with their concerns, struggles, and joys. Look for ways to encourage them as God gives you insight to do so. Get to know people you already know from work, school, or your neighborhood. Contact people in your address book and take them out to lunch. Where the relationship becomes relaxed, authentic, and mutual, make time for those friendships to grow so his community can take shape around you.

Seventh, let God expand your view of his church.

Most people think of the church as a specific group or meeting at a set time and place, and if you're not there, you are not part of his church. They are made to feel guilty and isolated as others withdraw from them. It's easy to feel as if you're the only one weary of the religious institution. But you're not. The latest research shows you are one in about thirty-one million adults in America who do not belong to a local congregation but are still actively looking to follow Christ, which is about the same number of people who do belong. That means one in every seven adults is on a similar journey to yours, and there are seven million who are "almost Dones," those who still attend but are there in body only.

Does that mean the church is failing? Only if we look at our human attempts to manage it. What you'll discover is that Jesus' church was never meant to be an institution, but a growing family who is learning to walk with him and who is learning to share his life and love with others. Real community flows from friendships, not meetings, which is why Jesus spent time with the people in his life in more informal settings. As we come to see his church as a reality outside of human control, then you can embrace her reality however she takes shape in the relationships and connections around you.

Learning to live in his freedom and joy is the fruit of a process that takes a significant period of time in our lives. Don't rush the process. Learn to embrace him and relax in the process, and you will discover that "something more" that your heart has been seeking. You'll find yourself in meaningful conversations that will deepen your own faith and encourage others to find more reality in theirs.

It is my hope that those who are done with religious institutions don't go off and create their own, but learn to live differently in the world. Then they'll be able to see the church Jesus is building taking shape right around them.

CHAPTER 10

. . . .

THE LABELS THAT DIVIDE US

In an article titled "Nones on the Rise" in 2012, Pew Research put out their findings that a growing segment of the US population now checks "none" as their religious preference, instead of one of the historic faiths that people have identified with for centuries.

It was perhaps inevitable then that the rise of the "Nones" would give rise to the "Dones," when it was discovered that there is an increasing number of people living outside traditional "church" institutions who continue to grow in a relationship with Jesus and connect in meaningful ways with others. The Dones is the most recent label attached to them. They have been called revolutionaries, outside the box, free-range Christians, or the dechurched. Such labels serve the media's need to talk about trends among specific groups and for others to market products inside those trends, but they really aren't helpful to the work Jesus is doing in the world.

Our fallen nature constantly seeks to find identity and safety inside a tribe, and labels are important to keep "my group" separate from "their group." It works for sports teams, gangs, and even religious groups. Labels so easily polarize humanity into adversaries, and especially with religious ones where we conclude that our group is not just different, but closer to God.

So, it's not surprising that labels either flatter or denigrate, depending on which tribe is talking. Sadly, most of this conversation about the Dones is either insiders talking to insiders about outsiders, or outsiders talking to outsiders about insiders. For insiders, terms like "dechurched" or "church refugees" may seem fair, but actually perpetuate the myth that religious institutions are the only reflection of Jesus' church in the world. That is as unfortunate as it is untrue. Using "church" only for religious institutions is no minor slip. Most religious leaders want people to believe it so they won't consider leaving, too. Even many of the so-called Dones talk about having "left the church."

Likewise, those outside want to claim the titles that make them seem freer, more grace-based, or more powerful than their counterparts in more traditional settings. After George Barna published *Revolution* in 2006, those outside of traditional structures quickly latched on to it as evidence that they were more spiritually committed, and instead of opening a dialog for the whole family, it only expanded the divide. "The Dones" will do the same thing if people wear it as a merit badge of deeper spirituality, while others use it to question the sincerity of their faith.

Any title you wear, be it pastor, bestselling author, or Done, will do more to separate you from others than it will help you recognize the incredible family that Jesus is building. Claiming a label works against his prayer that his Father would make us one. The community of the new creation levels our humanity—from hierarchy and from our narcissistic notions of being in a better group than others. We are all sons and daughters of a gracious Father and that's all the identity we need (Matthew 23:5-12).

But once again, we risk being divided into "innies" and "outies" and falling into the false dichotomy our flesh so craves. Whether you go to "a church" or whether you don't is a distinction without a difference. What matters is whether people are following Jesus and being transformed by his love. What I hope comes out of this study of the so-called "Dones" is those inside and those out recognize that the church is bigger than most of us would dare to believe, and that his church takes expression wherever people engage each other with his love and purpose.

For those who claim that attendance at a local congregation is mandatory to be part of his church, I hope they reconsider that false idea. Being part of his family is about following him, not belonging to an institution. Over the last twenty years I've found incredible followers of Jesus both inside them and outside. I hope this research draws all those into a conversation where in and out becomes less important than loving and affirming his kingdom, however it takes shape in the world. But it will take a significant number of voices across the Christian landscape to fight for a better conversation than those we usually have.

I am convinced that people who truly know Jesus will want to reach across this divide, not exacerbate it. We don't need identifying labels, especially ones that make us feel superior to others in the family. When Jesus becomes more important to us than finding identity in any particular tribe of it, then the conversations that most express his kingdom will grow in the world. Instead of demanding that others conform to our view of the church, we will recognize her in the most surprising places as we find connection and fellowship with those who know the Jesus we know, even if they don't follow the rituals we follow.

Then we won't need labels to divide us. Brother, sister, and fellow saint will be more than enough identity for each of us, and loving each other in a mutual celebration of Jesus himself will allow his church to flourish where we live.

CHAPTER 11

. . . .

DRAWING A LINE WHERE LINES DON'T HAVE TO BE DRAWN

"When I told my friends I'd left the church, they didn't want to talk to me anymore."

I can't tell you how many times I've had that conversation with people who are completely surprised that formerly close friends would so suddenly cut them off. The decision to leave a faith community after many years of service and with many friendships is rarely made in haste or with joy. It is usually born out of prolonged pain and frustration. Statistics show that most who have left did everything they could *not* to reach that conclusion. They tried to be a voice for change, but were pegged as complainers. When that failed, they tried to hunker down, ignore the things that disturbed them, and focus on the positives.

But their attempts didn't work. The final straw is rarely the most significant one. It's simply the one that made them realize they couldn't go on like this any longer. Whether it was the last manipulative sermon or announcement from the pulpit, political intrigue they could no longer ignore, or simple exhaustion from wrestling with concerns no one else there seemed to share, they finally come to a resolute decision because their conscience could not do otherwise. Of course, they want their closest friends to understand, even if they don't agree or aren't ready to make the same decision. They assume their friends will be interested in that journey, but once they begin to talk about it they are treated as a pariah. Because religious performance has schooled them in living for the approval of others, their desire to be understood comes off as a bit too passionate, and often too sharp.

Because Christianity, however, focuses on right versus wrong, many reach that decision by concluding something is wrong there and they have to leave. Thus, they are doing the "right" thing and those who do not support them are doing the "wrong" one. They may load up on Internet articles damning religious institutions as the harlot of Babylon, or blame a key leader or contributor as the leaven infecting the whole loaf who ruined it for them. They make their quest a moral one and see anyone opposing them as no longer following the truth.

The stage is set for intense conflict, and all the more because of their treasured friendships and their productive history with the congregation. The dialog of departure is too threatening to the future of the congregation to let it happen unchecked. Their story quickly finds its way into the ears of the leaders, who realize the inherent danger of discontent spreading throughout the congregation. It's amazing how quickly they can circle the wagons by marginalizing any malcontents with gossip and innuendo. There's nothing more threatening to the viability of any group of people than people leaving it, especially when they have a compelling explanation and long-term friendships. They have to characterize your decision as theologically wrong, and the gossip that ensues is intended to destroy your reputation and make people afraid to engage you. Doing so may say more about their fear of leadership than their lack of love for you.

So, on the one hand you have people making tortured decisions, wanting others to understand that decision and perhaps to even join them, and on the other, a group of people who feel judged and wounded by that decision and don't feel so friendly. My experience says that both sides wait for the other to make the first move, and both will wait for years. "I left six months ago and not one person has called me." Or, "They just vanished one day as if our friendship had no meaning to them."

No, that doesn't happen everywhere. There are congregations and pastors secure enough to let people have their journey, and if they no longer fit in, still treat them with kindness and generosity. However, I don't get email from people leaving those fellowships. I get it from those who are either harassed as someone who has rejected God, or ostracized as if they were some kind of virus. The latter is part of their attempt to get you to admit you're wrong and come back. In their minds they do it for your own good. This is how they "love" you, by withholding their friendship until you conform again.

This is a treacherous time for all concerned. Like me, you may need to take some distance from religious obligation to find freedom from it. Because I performed well, I could easily get sucked into that way of thinking if I hung around others who were pursuing it. To get away from it and have the time to cultivate new relationships not so mired in it was incredibly helpful for me. But I never lost my heart for those I'd left behind.

They were only doing what I had done for years, and rather than condemn them for it, I wanted to stay in touch with them in case a similar hunger got the better of them as well. And I discovered that as I learned to live inside the Father's affection, it became easier to be around performance-based people and not be drawn back onto the treadmill again.

People often ask me if there's a way to leave a congregation without hurting others. Of course, there's nothing we can do that will guarantee how people will respond, but as I've watched people go through this process for over two decades, I've discovered there are ways you can make it easier on yourself and others you care about.

Leave quietly. Unless Jesus clearly asks you to make some kind of last stand, and let people know that you're leaving and why, find a quieter exit. And if you do feel called to lay down the gauntlet, pray again to make sure you're not just misreading your own desire for personal vindication as the leading of the Spirit. The more hurt or betrayal you feel from others, the more your flesh will want to respond this way. Doing so, however, will burn bridges Jesus may still want you to cross.

Remember how long it took for you to see through the problems and come to the conclusions you have. Give time for the Spirit to do the same for them. You cannot make a clearer statement than simply withdrawing your participation; you need not beat them over the head with your reasons. One of the best books I've read on the subject is *A Tale of Three Kings* by Gene Edwards. His advice is to leave quietly without trying to take anyone with you. Let God deal with their hearts. If people ask you what's going on, don't make "last-stand statements" about leaving the horrible "institutional church" to follow Jesus more freely. Be gently honest if you have the relationship, but don't expect them to understand.

Talk about it in ways that impart grace to the hearer. When you find others who are done with the traditional congregation, you can talk freely, encourage each other's journeys, and work out your frustrations at how the system may have hurt you. With those who are still in it, however, it is far better to speak more gently, leaving a door open if they want to explore it more, not trying to force your conclusions on them before they are ready to hear.

Don't try so hard to be understood and don't cast aspersions on other people or leadership. Of course, I'm not encouraging you to be dishonest. If there is real corruption in the leadership or dynamics in the congregation others need to be warned about, do it cautiously. However, you don't have to tell people everything and overwhelm them with your hurts. Just let them know you're reconsidering some things in a prayerful season. If they're interested they will ask for more, but discern those who are genuinely hungry and caring from those who just want to hear some gossip to feed the rumor mill.

It is not your job to convince others that what you're doing is the right response against injustice or evil. Laying out all your frustrations may well damage the relationship and force them to make a judgment about you when they don't even understand what you're doing. In many cases, you probably don't understand all that's going on yet either, even in your own heart.

Be careful what you share on social media. Not everyone in your pool of relationships will appreciate being confronted with your journey every day. Many people early in this journey take out their frustrations on others by wrapping their story in newfound controversial theological views they know will be a poke in the eye to people in their family and their former congregation. They seem to need the validation of being provocative and enduring other people's reactions. In time, they will come to see that though it makes them feel as if they're doing something important, they are actually alienating people whom Jesus also loves. Many of these will complain about the loss of friends they've suffered and play the martyr role in their search for truth, but they have only brought it on themselves.

There's nothing valuable about working out your issues in a public space, and it only invites greater hurt. This is best done in personal conversations with people who've been down that road already and can listen, understand, and help you think through where some of your thoughts might lead. You will discover that your views will shift dramatically over time, and that the closer you come to his truth, you will discover a huge helping of gentleness and humility that can encourage others without attacking them. Being antagonistic doesn't open people to your point of view or to the God you're learning to love, but caring about them as people on a journey will.

Avoid drawing the hard line.

If people ask where you've been, instead of telling them you've left the Institutional Church never to return again, think again. That may be how you feel today, but grace is best tasted with daily bites. You may feel the need to leave now, but you don't know where this journey will take you or how God might lead you down the road. Who knows if God might call you back into a more congregational environment for a number of reasons? You don't even know if the decision you're making is temporary or permanent.

The encouragements in Scripture about following Jesus focus on our daily response to him, as best we discern his leading. Making stands based on some newfound conclusions or what you think is "right" versus what is "wrong" doesn't usually stand the test of time anyway. By stating them too early, you paint yourself into a corner that you may not end up wanting to defend. Transformation of our thinking and our living takes place over time and we can't possibly guess today what we might know better years from now.

Those who have left their congregations causing the least amount of damage and maintaining many of their friendships didn't draw such hard lines. Instead they talked about needing a sabbatical or a taking a break from the activities that have exhausted them so they can once again focus on their relationship with Jesus. They may tell people they're considering what the church is and how best for them to engage her in this season of their life. The more you personalize God's leading, the less they will need to feel rejected. I've often told people who ask me where I go to church that I no longer attend a specific congregation, but I am exploring more relational ways of doing church. That has opened doors for many a thoughtful and sensitive conversation. If you need to resign from leadership positions or other responsibilities, do it directly and kindly. Keep in mind you don't owe anyone an explanation no matter how badly they want one. Just tell them that you're convinced this is what God has for you at this time. It's hard to argue with that.

Make your decision seem less final and less judgmental by seeing it as a season in your life in which God might be shifting your priorities or perceptions. The less threatening you make it, the more people will be able to care about you instead of choosing sides. That is the best way for you to see it as well. How many times have we made ironclad decisions for life that turned out to be wrong? We are all growing, all learning to follow him, and it's best for us to see that as leading in the moment, rather than new rules to live by for the rest of our lives.

If they are interested they will ask for more and even then, be sensitive to how much you share. Where they are genuinely concerned, open up more freely. Where they become defensive, back off a bit. This is about caring for them, not feeding your need to be right.

Realize new relationships will not come easily.

Many people think they will leave their congregation and suddenly discover a lot of people ready to fellowship in more relational ways. Unfortunately, that's not usually the case. Many congregations are so ingrown that people have few other quality friendships beyond their borders.

Once you've left, what are you going to do to find new relationships? If you just think your congregation is fatally flawed, you may want to try some others to see if they are less so. Many take this option and find their way into larger congregations where they can just put in their time and be less conspicuous. Those who have the most success here usually go to smaller congregations closer to home, and find people to love rather than a program to entertain them.

But for those who are really giving up on religious obligation and want to find more relational connections, don't think finding a new group or even new friendships will be easy. You'll want to find people of "like mind," and if you do that will be helpful, but the best friendships don't come out of finding people who are already like you, but growing in friendships through your differences. Look to love whomever is before you, rather than trying to find a group of people on the same journey, and it will be less frustrating.

Many find this a lonely season, especially if they made their decision alone, but that isn't bad either. Loneliness is often not about the lack of other people, but our lack of connection with Jesus. This is a great time to get to know him and learn to rest in his love, so new friendships can grow more without loneliness twisting them to your preferred ends.

Be a force for greater unity.

Jesus' most passionate prayer for his followers is that we'd all be brought to complete unity. If you're finding your way out of the traditional congregation, don't be shy about loving people who still go. If they are open to friendship without either of you trying to "fix" the other, pursue it. Keep the conversation on "Jesus" instead of "church" and you'll find more fruitful conversations.

As you find more freedom in his love, you'll find their guilt and condemnation will have no place to land. You can even expose it gently and honestly, even humorously, and those who really care about you will learn to lay it down, at least in your presence. And they will when they see it no longer impacts you. They may want that freedom for themselves, but let them ask. That doesn't mean you have to hang out with toxic people who try to put their bondage on you, but you will be able to love more freely those lost in the darkness.

Just don't try to get people to see what you see. Trust the Spirit to do that as you simply enjoy them where they are on their own journey. In doing so you'll fulfill the heart of the Father for increased love and affection. Some even find themselves once again in traditional congregations, but as very different people who are no longer playing the same religious and political games.

Don't forget to love.

The real freedom from religious obligation comes as we learn to live in his love, rather than create a new set of obligations to get others to follow. That even includes people we disagree with and those who mistreat us. That takes time, however, and be careful not to turn love into another obligation. Learn to love from the heart and don't force yourself to live beyond your own freedom. As I said above, you may initially need to take some distance from those who hold you in judgment or try to manipulate you, even family members. But that will change over time.

As you discover how much he loves you, that relationship will transform everything about the way you see him, see yourself, and see others. You'll increasingly find yourself disconnected from obligation and the ability to be manipulated by guilt or fear. You'll be able to be around others, even those who disagree with your journey, and not be influenced by their angst.

It's a tough lesson to be sure, but one that will reap great rewards. If we try to force others to our own conclusions, we're playing the same game of conformity and manipulation that they are. Love doesn't press; it entreats. It cares for someone, looking for the conversation that may bring light when people are ready.

And that goes for all of us. So, whether your place in the journey has you inside an established congregation, or learning to live in the joy of his church outside of them, we'd all do well to treat each other with love and grace. Our unity will never come agreeing on all the finer points of doctrine or observing the same practices, but by caring about each other in spite of our differences and looking for ways to encourage others to draw more closely to Jesus.

Live true to his work in you and be generous with others, and you'll fulfill all he has in mind for you. You'll also be a blessing to his wider church in the world.

. . . .

CHAPTER 12

REACHING ACROSS THE GROWING DIVIDE

So, we have thirty-one million passionate followers of Jesus who regularly attend a Sunday gathering, and many of them believe local congregations are the only place a true believer can engage the church of Jesus Christ today. And we have thirty-one million passionate followers of Jesus who no longer belong to a recognized congregation, and many of them believe that corporations are a poor reflection of the church Jesus came to build.

So, who is right?

Neither.

And the fact that they both think they are and look down on the others tears the very fabric on which the church of Jesus Christ is sewn together. Nothing in Scripture, including Hebrews 10:25, obligates us to arrange ourselves in institutional settings, and nothing in Scripture says that God can't be among those who do, to share his glory and invite them into his reality. So, whether you "go to church" or whether your friend doesn't is not important to God. The sooner it no longer matters to you, the freer you'll be able to love whomever God wants you to love and walk with.

How we define the church is not of first importance to Jesus, but whether we are engaged with him and his work in the world. Arguing over church issues is like two teams showing up in the aftermath of a landslide to save those who are trapped, and instead of jumping to the task at hand, they begin to argue over who has the better brand of rescue equipment.

Senseless, isn't it?

Paul said, "The only thing that counts is faith expressing itself in love" (Galatians 5:6). The Galatians fought over circumcision; we do it over Sunday attendance. In the end, neither matters. What does matter is a growing trust in our Father expressed by the love we share for others. Participating in a local congregation does not save you, and not participating in one does not damn you, even if others claim so. There are lots of ways to get quality teaching, find meaningful fellowship, and participate in the kingdom coming in the world, and doing it through a local congregation is only one of those. If you find it helpful and meaningful to your faith, be there, and if not, look for other ways to connect with people more relationally.

But now, more than ever, we need to reach across whatever we think divides us and do the one thing that Jesus asked us to do as his followers: Love one another as he loves us, and that includes people with whom you have differences. In fact, loving others has mostly to do with our differences; it's easy to love people who think like we do. We fall into the same trap Jesus' disciples did when they saw others doing miracles that weren't part of their discipleship group. Jesus warned them to have a more expansive view of the kingdom and a more generous view of people: "Whoever is not against us is for us."

We've been divided long enough by brand names, rituals, doctrine, and denominational structures. Isn't it time we found a different reality to recognize the church Jesus is building around us? Even if you attend a local congregation, you would miss a lot of what God is doing in the world if you think it the only expression of Christ's church in your community or the world, or that they are the only people God wants you to know.

For the past twenty years, I've walked alongside people who've lost connection with and hope in institutional Christianity. They haven't, however, lost their faith in Jesus, their passion for real community with other disciples, or their desire to touch the world around them. They are discovering that church life doesn't require an institutional component. During that time, I have also kept up friendships with people who swear by the necessity of those local congregations. I have close relationships with people who are elders, pastors, and committed attenders, who have provided great encouragement and wisdom for my journey. I have been involved with a number of outreaches to the poor and marginalized in the communities in which I've lived, some sponsored by denominations and others by individuals with a passion to serve their community.

The body of Christ has become so much larger and far more diverse for me, filled with people who wouldn't agree with everything I believe, but they do share a relationship with the same Father I know. What draws us together is not our theology about church, but finding ourselves alongside each other in the river of the Father's affection. In that connection, the sheer silliness of whether or not someone attends a specific meeting regularly is seen for what it is. When we make doctrine or religious practice the basis of church life we only add to the division. Most of those differences are not based on the essentials of who Christ is anyway, but on our varying interpretations of obscure passages that become less important in the face of love.

All I need to have fellowship with you is to have the slightest inkling that you are getting to know the Father I know. I recognize that by the love he's pouring into your heart, both for him and for others, and especially for those who don't see the world the way you do. Are you learning to be generous and kind, or becoming more judgmental, demanding that others agree with you? You can be one day old in this faith with all kinds of doctrinal suppositions askew, and no idea how to live in his reality, and yet we can share life because that life is in him, not the correctness of our doctrine. In time, he will bring you and me closer to what's true. That's why I don't regard conformity a condition for fellowship or collaboration. All I need to see is a Father's love growing in your life. I trust him to take care of the rest.

Sara and I have been reading a fascinating book called *The Soul of Shame* by Dr. Curt Thompson, MD, who uses brain science to show the devastating effects of shame that disconnects our brain functions internally as well as our relationships externally. Shame, whether in the form of self-pity or arrogance, shatters the creation and isolates us from others. He writes, "Shame has a way of translating *different* into *better* or *worse*. To the degree that shame has a foothold in my heart, I can unconsciously react to difference with judgment directed either at the other or myself."

If love were the most important thing, we would be able to walk together and put his love in the world without being threatened by people who live out their faith differently than we do. I'm not suggesting that there isn't right and wrong thinking about God, because there is. I'm just harkening back to Romans 14, where Paul invites us not to try to shape each other's journey, but trust God's Spirit to do that. "If there are corrections to be made or manners to be learned, God can handle that without your help" (Romans 14:4, MSG). And the best environment for that to happen is where people are being loved and cared for, while they are being encouraged to get to know Jesus better.

A long time ago, I gave up the need to classify someone by their denominational affiliation or lack of it, or even use it as a gauge of the depth of their spiritual passion. Love doesn't require it and doing so only chokes the hope of relationship. Scripture does not empower any entity called "the church" to determine who is a part of God's kingdom and who isn't. We have too long worried about drawing the lines to determine who belongs to God, enforcing those lines with a vigor that snuffs out the smoldering wick and snaps off the bruised reed.

Paul entrusted that work elsewhere. "God's solid foundation stands firm, sealed with this inscription: 'The Lord knows those who are his'" (2 Timothy 2:19). If he knows, we don't have to. Jesus had already warned his apostles that if they tried to separate the wheat from the weeds, they would destroy the wheat in the process (Matthew 13).

What would happen if all we looked for in each other was a growing participation in the reality of his love and sharing it with others? Wouldn't we find better connection with brothers and sisters around us, regardless of what group they belong to or what doctrinal differences we had? Wouldn't this be the fruit of the Spirit Jesus encouraged us to look for, rather than some man's wisdom, or some woman's seeming miracle-working power?

If we're going to be the people in whom Jesus' prayer for "complete unity" is fulfilled, we're going to have to put him and his love in the preeminent place, and nothing else. We're going to have to get over being threatened by people who see life differently, and worry less about those who claim we can't be followers of Christ because we don't jump through whatever hoop they think is essential.

We respond to his Spirit as he knits the church together by pursuing those relationships he puts on our heart. For local church advocates, you would be blessed to reach beyond the borders of their own institution, connect with Christians in other groups, and share fellowship with those who don't attend at all. For those who've stopped attending, you'll be blessed to have connections with those who still do, if they will allow it and not despise your journey.

Jesus' family in your locale is so much bigger than the ways we've divided her up. How much more would we demonstrate the kingdom if we loved and cooperated beyond our different views of church or our doctrinal distinctions? Love can do that. Nothing else can.

Of course, not everyone is going to see the church this way. Many will hold to their rituals and doctrines as hills to die on, judging harshly those who do not do the same. But what we need is an increasing number of Jesus-followers learning to love generously, reaching across our imagined lines of demarcation, and loving and serving alongside others Jesus has invited us to know.

If we let this relational reality that love allows define the church, it will free us to love other followers of Christ with open hearts and hands. Recently, along with a group of pastors and those who see church beyond the local congregation, I was invited to dialog about my book, *Finding Church*. At the very end, one pastor spoke up and said, "I know a 'Done' who used to be a close friend and elder but left my congregation five years ago. How should I treat him?"

My heart melted at the question. I've been a pastor. I know how painful it is to have good friends leave the fellowship. Most don't even mean it personally, but that doesn't mean we don't take it that way. It always felt like a personal rejection of me, my message, or at least the friendship we shared together. But this man wanted to reach beyond that pain and see if the friendship was still there.

I found myself responding, "If you cared about him then, why wouldn't he be your friend now? I'd take him out for coffee and just reconnect, focusing the conversation on Jesus instead of church." He did exactly that. By the time I'd driven the two hours it took me to get home, I had a voice mail from that pastor. He'd called his friend right after the meeting, and since he was available, he drove straight to a coffee shop to meet him. They hadn't seen each other in five years, but his voice cracked as he shared the amazing conversation they had: "I have my best friend back."

Wouldn't it be great if our friendships could grow regardless of what we might be doing differently on Sunday morning? More than nailing down the holes in someone else's doctrine, or spending countless hours in religious activity, we would simply learn to live in the ever-growing reality of his love. If fellowship really spreads like this, our tribal distinctions will become meaningless and Jesus' prayer that all his followers will be one would be answered.

It may only take a phone call, but in such moments the kingdom of God grows in the world.

. . . .

CHAPTER 13

DO YOU HAVE
COMMUNITY?

The question is as ubiquitous as it is silly: "What church do you go to?"

It's almost always the first thing Christians ask each other when they meet, and it is the most divisive question in all Christendom. We think identifying the particular tribe of Christian someone belongs to will tell us a lot about them. Are they Calvinist, Catholic, charismatic, Bible thumpers, high church or fundamentalist?

The truth is, it tells us very little about people. It is an overly simplistic way to profile people with our stereotypical view of any group, while it tells us nothing about them as individuals. It doesn't tell us how deeply they are connected to Jesus, or whether they are thriving on their spiritual journey or withering away in despair. While the question causes some to swell with pride in their particular movement, others are apprehensive for the judgment their answer might incur.

For the thirty-one million Christians in America who are following Jesus but no longer attend a formal congregation, answering that question is a dilemma. If you say you don't, many will question the sincerity of your faith, convinced that all true Christians belong to a local congregation. They make no room for a vibrant faith and an engaging experience of church life without the institutional map.

Recently someone I was just getting to know asked me that question as he was feeling me out for some potential collaboration. When my answer wasn't satisfactory he asked a second question, "Do you have a community where you live?" I knew he was giving me a chance to redeem myself by assuring him I belonged to some kind of Christian group, even if I wasn't calling it "a church."

I wasn't trying to be difficult. We had just met and he was desperate to find some kind of box to fit me into that would allow him to affirm the validity of my faith. He could only do that if I belonged to a group with a name, a regular (hopefully weekly) meeting, and a specified doctrine.

I didn't want to mislead him, but I tend to use words like this with intentional precision. I don't have a community; I have three pools of relationships that I explore life in Jesus with locally and even more globally. None of them is an organized group with names and leadership structures. Some think that means they don't count, but they would be wrong. I see community very differently than he did, and I knew we weren't going to get through this on his terminology alone.

"Why don't you ask me if I have community where I live?" I offered.

That stopped him. He looked quizzically for a second and

then asked what I meant. Now we were having the conversation I hoped to have. Yes, I have community, more of it than I had ever experienced in any congregation I'd been a part of. None of these have coalesced into a named group or regular routine, but the relationships intersect frequently and among those I am deeply known, have people to love and serve, and am regularly challenged to an ever-deepening engagement with Jesus.

He got the point. People can belong to "a community" without having community. The biggest complaint I hear from people who attend a congregation is that few relationships seem to get beneath the surface of people's lives. Our culture uses the term "community" for any social group that shares a common interest or structure. When I think of community, however, I don't think of regular meetings, standardized conduct, or a superintending leadership structure. I think of deep friendships where people are known without pretense and where they share mutual love, encouragement, and serve each other as a normal part of their everyday lives.

It is the innate hunger for these kinds of friendships that is causing people to look beyond our large, tired institutions. Instead of incubating close, personal, caring relationships, many foster a conformity-based culture where meeting a set of religious expectations subverts the genuineness out of which community grows. The political realities of running an institution, and people going along with those, subvert the hope of real community. When you're pretending to be what you're not to be loved and accepted, real relationship won't happen. People don't know you; they only know who you pretend to be.

Community can't be manufactured by human programming; it is the fruit of people living authentically and lovingly with an expanding pool of growing friendships that defies age, interests, ethnicity, and societal status. Community is the fruit of people connecting with others beneath the masks we often wear to negotiate society. It's real concern, real affection, and real honesty inside a growing relationship with Jesus.

You can't have community with everyone sitting in a large auditorium, nor by working together on the "church program." It may happen in those settings, but not because of those things; it's because people connect in growing friendships beyond them—before and after the meetings, in conversations, meals and activities where people can relax and be themselves.

That's why I prefer the question, "Do you have community?" Are there people around you who know the real you—your hopes and dreams, doubts and fears? Are they willing to struggle with you as you learn to follow Jesus and be open with their own lives as well? Can you freely ask questions, and struggle with the questions of life and faith? Are they people you are delighted to see when they come around?

These are all reflections of real community, and few people have such friendships. Most of our human interactions, especially in our shame and desire to control others, undermine that reality. Religious environments often trigger those responses, and rather than letting people relax into a relationship that's real, they try to force one through pretense.

So how do you find community? This is as true for people who go to an organized gathering as those who do not. Real community has to be found at its source—inside the Trinity itself. Father, Son, and Spirit share the most breathtaking dance of community in the universe. Their love for each other is rich and full, and because of that they are able to share life, glory, trust, and truth in such an awesome way that it is difficult for us to conceive of it in the brokenness of the creation. But we are invited to participate in it. Jesus said to his disciples, "On that day you will realize that I am in my Father, and you are in me, and I am in you" (John 14:20).

Jesus invited us into the relationship the Trinity shares together. As we grow in our awareness of them and learn to love and trust them the same way they trust each other, we will begin to experience the wonder of their community. That happens as we learn to rest in their love and watch as they make themselves known in us. Jesus showed us how that happened as he walked along the road with his disciples or relaxed in Mary and Martha's home in Bethany.

And as we get increasingly comfortable inside the Divine community, we will find ourselves quite naturally sharing it with others. The shame that sabotages our relationships and drives us to pretense and performance will begin to fade away, and we'll find that we are more compassionate for people and freer to care about them. That's where you find community, not by looking to be loved, but by beginning to love others.

The love we desire from others is the love we first give away even without any expectation of return. God wants his love to envelop people even if they never respond to it. But when they do, and are able to reach back in loving ways toward you, a friendship is born. It is out of friendship that community begins. And, no, this doesn't happen quickly. It takes time to get to know people, hear their story, and sense that connection that can become a friendship, and then we need the proximity to let that relationship grow. We are too quick to form groups and try to trust each other when many are still so broken that they have no idea how to love. The results can be devastating as people feel used or as competition or gossip takes hold.

Some are so broken that they will pretend to love you, as long as they benefit from you. When they no longer do, they will cut you off or even worse, betray you to gain a foothold with others. It happened to Jesus, too, so we dare not think ourselves immune from it. But don't let that keep you from exploring the relationships love can build. Just keep on loving the way you are loved by him. In time, you'll find yourself alongside others who also know how to love beyond their own self-interest. Don't let hurt draw you back into yourself. Evil has a way of fragmenting relationships, but his love allows us to overcome the immaturity of others and keep loving them if possible, or move on from them if not.

Our engagement with others need not go any deeper than how safely we are exploring life with them. We are won into friendships; they cannot be imposed on us. And even healthy community will have its ups and downs. We live in a fallen world and our expressions of community will be flawed as well. Don't expect others to always get it right, and don't put that demand on yourself. There's a lot of forgiveness and forbearance in any friendship that thrives over time. In real community, loving each other is more important than being right or trying to fix others to meet our expectations.

Community is about friendships and it enhances all of life, where we live, work and play. Not all our friends have to be followers of Jesus. By caring about others and letting them care about you, you provide the fertile ground where sharing the kingdom takes place. If you are graceful with them, many will come to know the God you know, and then the friendships only deepen.

Community rises out of the friendships God gives you, and as you are generous with those friendships, a living network of friends and friends of friends will emerge around you. Some may be local, others from further away. The best gift I can give my friends is to introduce them to my other friends. That growing network of interconnected friends will overlap with other expressions as a tapestry of God's church makes itself known in the world.

Having community is a way to live. We have to make time for friendships, space for new people, and learn to love people simply as they are, not how we would like them to be. We are not alone here. It is Jesus' job to build the church and the Spirit's task to show us our place in it. This relational way of engaging his church is a challenge to be sure, but the fruits of doing so are to experience an ever-growing network of friendships that brings wisdom, healing, comfort, and joy to your life in Jesus.

CHAPTER 14

. . . .

AN INVITATION,
NOT AN IMPOSITION

Shortly after the research on the exodus of the so-called "Dones" was released, I was invited to participate on a panel that presented the statistics of those leaving traditional congregations and to share my experience of being with people who no longer see the church as an institution. "The Future of the Church Summit" was designed to help pastors wrestle with the fact that so many people are leaving traditional congregations, and statistics showed there is little hope of getting them back. The question they hoped to answer was, "How do we keep the ones we have from leaving too?"

It was a courageous attempt, but sadly the focus was on fixing the program. They focused on making worship more sensory and interactive, preaching shorter sermons and involving more stories from others (videotaped so you can edit out the boring bits), and more streamlined decision-making.

There was even one session on innovative new programs to help the church go out where the people are, instead of trying to get them to come to a building. That seemed promising. All five of the presenters started by telling a compelling story of how someone had a passion to reach people who had little desire for God. Each held that longing before God for a significant period of time, and then God gave them a task to do that proved wonderfully fruitful. You would think that would be a process worth encouraging. Instead, all of the presenters, after telling their story, tried to sell pastors on the program they created in its aftermath. Taking something lovely God had done, they systematized it into what they hoped would be a replicable program, put it in a book, and were peddling their new system, completely omitting how it had all begun.

Surprisingly, not one session dared to ask if God were in this and if so, how we might celebrate and participate with him. All assumed that the "rise of the Dones" was bad news and it needed to be fixed by once again tweaking the program. My experience assures me that those who have given up on traditional congregations aren't looking for a better program or system to implement. They have found them all to be short-lived, less fruitful than promised, and rather than leading to more authentic engagements with God and his church, actually produced systems needing continual maintenance and relationships that never reached beneath the surface. Instead of seeking out new programs, we could instead answer the deeper cry of the heart that longs to know God and walk in his ways.

To that end, programs are part of the problem. They only prop up an otherwise thin reality... until they fail. Then what? Programs are an imposition. Someone sets up the doctrine we must believe, the rituals we must observe, or the curriculum we must follow and then seeks to conform others to it, often with a system of rewards and punishments that manipulates people through obligation and guilt. No matter how well intentioned these systems are, they are still an attempt to force an outside, artificial construct on this amazing adventure of life. Instead of drawing people into God's life, these only alienate them from it, either because they don't understand it or do not see the fruits they were promised.

Could this be why Jesus didn't give his disciples any list of doctrines, rituals, or discipleship workbooks to share with others? Instead he spoke of a better kingdom where God's love and power works within them. He invited a handful of them into that same reality, both by modeling it for them and by showing them how they could participate in it too. He wasn't imposing a system of living from the outside, but helping them rethink from the inside how it is to connect with God's reality and to follow him freely. It took over three years to help them even begin to learn how to live in the Father's love and freely share it with others.

Perhaps the greatest lesson here is that the life of God can't be imposed; that's the stuff of religion. You can get people to follow systems and confess true doctrines, but without a change in the heart they will never connect with him and find a trajectory that will lead them to increasing life and freedom. The Incarnation taught us that God doesn't draw a line in the sand and tell us to cross it, but shows up where we actually are—lost in our doubts, our fears, and our lies—and invites us into a process of transformation as our relationship with him grows. Without that, people will simply pretend as best they can until the frustration of their own emptiness wins out.

That's what is happening with many who are giving up on religious systems today, while their hunger for God still grows. For years they did everything asked of them and still did not find the life in God they had been promised. They thought they were the only one struggling with the failures of this system, and are only now finding out they are not. They know there is "something more" out there and have set out to find it, and they are not hopeful that yet another program will do it.

That's why many are leaving and why I applaud that passion. We've had enough of prepackaged programs, cookie-cutter discipleship curricula where one size does not fit all. The congregations that will survive this season will not try to overhaul the program, but will find a more generous way to help people discover the reality behind our faith—God himself! They won't look at the "Dones" as fallen brothers and sisters, but as colleagues in the faith setting out in uncharted waters to find a city whose architect and builder is God.

Discipleship can only work when it is an invitation to a hungry heart, not by imposing the way people should act or think from the outside. So instead of investing our time coming up with new programs, writing yet another curriculum, or enforcing a ritual to follow, we would be better served to come alongside people who are hungry and help them discover how God is already at work in them. We can encourage them to recognize and to follow what he has already put in their heart. His life is a journey to discover, not a program to complete.

"Come to me," Jesus offered. That's the invitation. Come if you want; obligation won't work here. Yield to a relationship with him that will reorder everything you think and every way you respond to others in life. That takes time to grow in the heart so you're not just following a list of good ideas, but actually living differently. Those who have met God in that way know there is no program that can replicate it. Life is too varied, and our humanity too unique, to convey to the rigidity of a program.

It's something he wants to sort out in each heart, and the best way we can help is not by organizing another seminar or summit, but by coming alongside people and helping them see what Jesus has already begun in them.

People responding freely to that invitation will help shape the future of the church as she makes herself known in this generation.

CHAPTER 15

. . . .

HAVE WE OVERPLAYED THE SERMON CARD?

I sat down to lunch with a good friend of mine one Tuesday afternoon, while I was still pastoring at a local congregation. We couldn't even get our order placed before he exploded with excitement over the sermon I had preached two days before. "That was the best sermon I've ever heard. It changed my life."

I knew it had gone well. Anyone who preaches regularly knows there are times when some sermons are just okay, and other times when everything comes together—the content, the crowd, a great illustration, even a move of the Spirit—that makes it incredibly special. That had been one of those times, but I was nonetheless intrigued by his last comment.

"Really? How did it change you?"

I could immediately see my question caught him off guard. In his eyes, I could see that his mind was churning, but nothing was coming out of his mouth except, "Ahh... Ahh... Ummm..." His lips had tightened and his fist pulsated in front of his chin, but he couldn't think of a thing to say.

I tried again. "Can you tell me one thing you took away from that sermon?"

"Let me think," he said, buying time. "Remind me again what you talked about."

"Oh no you don't," I responded playfully.

"At least give me the text," he pleaded. I shook my head. After a bit more silence, we both started to laugh. Only forty-eight hours after the best sermon he'd ever heard and he couldn't even remember what it was about.

This was one of those wake-up moments in my life. I used to love preaching sermons and having a roomful of people hang on my every word. I thrived on their laughter in response to a funny story or their wetted eyes when some truth touched their heart. I knew my friend was not given to flattery, for he was as apt to criticize as he was to compliment. That sermon had touched him powerfully, if not enduringly.

I had already grown suspicious that the Sunday sermon is one of the most ineffective ways to help people grow spiritually. I have seen good sermons go by before without having any impact on the people who heard it. I have binders full of notes from sermons and teachings I've heard, and while I can repeat the content of some of the more memorable ones, I can't say that any of them actually changed the trajectory of my life.

Strange, isn't it? It's one of the two most important reasons people go to Sunday services. One is for what many call worship, that time of singing, prayer, praise, or even celebrating the Eucharist, and the other is the sermon. Any serious Christian will have a regular dose of both, or so the prevailing thought is.

But how much time did Christ spend doing either? Did he ever teach his disciples how to facilitate a good "worship" experience, or how to craft a powerful sermon?

Perhaps we've overplayed the sermon card.

Looking back over the Gospels, I'm amazed at how few sermons he actually gave, and even when he did, how little impact it had on those who listened. Not one of them was ever scheduled in advance. He simply talked to whomever he was with, whether it be an afternoon with a Samaritan woman, or her friends and family later that night. It could be his disciples in a boat or 5,000 scattered on a hillside, but it was never a prepared text, a scripted lecture, or a flourishing finish with a well-thought-out application for the people to go and obey.

He talked about his Father's kingdom and how they could embrace it. He wasn't teaching doctrine, ethics, or rituals, but helping people discover how to live with God inside the reality of their own challenges. It was no wonder the most transformative moments came in personal conversations and why our preoccupation with sermons, seminars, and classes produces a Christianity that some complain is a mile wide but only an inch deep.

Fr. Richard Rohr recently wrote, "Christians have preferred to hear something Jesus never said: 'Worship me.' Worship of Jesus is rather harmless and risk-free; following Jesus changes everything." He went on to suggest that the Sunday teaching is "like a secret social contract between clergy and laity, as we shake hands across the sanctuary. We agree not to tell you anything that would make you uncomfortable, and you will keep coming to our services. It is a nice deal, because once the Gospel is preached, I doubt if the churches would be filled. Rather, we might be out on the streets living the message." He called it a codependent relationship that actually keeps the Gospel from spreading in the world.

This is one of the major reasons so many people are giving up on the Sunday morning delivery system. It is proving increasingly irrelevant to their spiritual lives. They can get good teaching in other places; what they need is less a Sunday morning pep talk to try harder and more of an exchange that is relevant to their own journey. They seek a vibrant spirituality that fulfills the promises they've heard about in sermon after sermon. To help them discover that, we need to move beyond lectures and books to the kind of encounters with people that Jesus had.

I got my pilot's license when I was seventeen. While I did attend ground school and learn all the intricacies of aerodynamics, navigation, weather, air traffic control, and how to load a balanced aircraft, I never learned to fly. That took climbing into an aircraft along with an instructor who could show me what to do to actually fly a plane. That could never happen in a class; it had to happen with a tutor.

So, I'm not saying that sermons have no value, only that the value is limited. They can provide valuable information and inspiration, but their impact on spiritual transformation is fairly weak, and all the more so as people get used to hearing the same voice each week. They may find it informative, inspirational, even entertaining, but at the end of the day it cannot show them how to live. For that they need a more mature friend with whom they can share their experiences, questions, and even doubts as they explore their own connection to God.

Listening to sermons, even taking notes and trying to live out the application, is probably the worst way to discover how to live inside the love of the Father and to follow him. I'm convinced that ninety percent of teaching and preaching occurs in a conversation where questions are being asked, doubts considered, and difficult realities contemplated. The life of Christ doesn't flow well in three-point outlines on a topic they are not even considering until I bring it up. Christ comes to them "in life," not far removed from it in the comfort of a sanctuary. Learning to live inside his reality is very different from learning the routines of Christianity as a religion.

Yes, I still talk to larger groups, but far less as a lecture and far more as a conversation that allows people to learn in their time and through their own experiences. What are their questions, doubts, and struggles, and how might I frame a question or observation that leads them into a wider world where God makes himself known to them? I've come to value the time in cars and homes with people far more than I do standing on a stage, and I see far more impact from it as well.

This kind of teaching enthralls me. Oh, it is more difficult than preparing a lecture on the topic of my choosing. It demands that I engage with them, listening carefully to their story and concerns with an ear tuned to the Spirit so that I can respond not with a pat answer, but with something tailored to them in that moment. After all, the life of Jesus isn't about teaching people a set of doctrines, but assisting them in finding their way into living in the growing awareness of his life.

Sermons give the mistaken idea that there is a well-crafted answer to every question, but that's only because we set up the question to fit our answers. The sermons can unwittingly intimidate people from engaging others with real questions because real conversations don't happen in outline form. The very positioning of a lecture sets up an expert in the front of the room whom everyone should listen to, rather than a fellow struggler in this amazing adventure of participating in the mystery of Christ in us.

In fact, it may be true that the one teaching the sermon gets the most value out of it. It usually is attached to his or her life, wrestling with content important for their journey. But if we want to serve others, wouldn't we want to reverse that? Instead of sharing what has value in our lives, we would be helping them with what makes the most sense in theirs.

Studying just to share a teaching and then rushing back to your study to prepare another doesn't even give time for it to sink in to your own life, much less theirs. I remember sharing on many topics that were fresh to my own journey, but as soon as I taught about them I moved on to something else that interested me, without embracing the very realities about which I was teaching.

Our preoccupation with sermons is built on the underlying assumption that we grow best by hearing a truth and then applying it to our lives. That may work for writing computer code or cleaning a home, but it will not teach people how to follow him. For that, they need an encounter with God in their unfolding circumstances and the insight to lean into his reality. It's not the preaching of the Scriptures we need more of, but the preaching of Christ that helps people see him in their own lives and follow him.

What we need are men and women living the life themselves, who can freely pass it on to others in conversation. Our emphasis on the Sunday sermon as the center of the local congregation and the focus for spiritual growth causes us to keep raising up generations of young men and women who are academically equipped to teach sermons, but are ill-prepared to be a companion alongside someone's spiritual journey. They can write an outline and talk with eloquence, but they have no idea how to help someone find a transformative relationship in the midst of the circumstances life throws at them.

In recent decades, an old word has re-emerged to describe this approach: spiritual director. The word places a greater emphasis on professionalism and control than I like and is often only available to the wealthy or well-connected. Can you imagine if older brothers and sisters who've been on the journey for a while would be willing to share their encouragement and wisdom without the authority and control that so easily sidetracks it? All you have to do is come alongside someone as a friend and share your journey and insights, allowing the Holy Spirit to help them see what's best for their journey.

The church in the West is not withering for lack of knowledge, but for a lack of knowing him and being transformed by him. We teach Christ as a religion to follow that is empty and futile, rather than helping people live it with freedom. The early church had the same problem. Paul wanted them to learn that it wasn't empty and futile. His admonishment in Colossians 2 is as applicable today as it was to his listeners:

> My counsel for you is simple and straightforward:
> Just go ahead with what you've been given. You
> received Christ Jesus, the Master; now *live* him.
> You're deeply rooted in him. You're well constructed
> upon him. You know your way around the faith.
> Now do what you've been taught. School's out; quit
> studying the subject and start *living* it! And let your
> living spill over into thanksgiving.

Watch out for people who try to dazzle you with big words and intellectual double-talk. They want to drag you off into endless arguments that never amount to anything. They spread their ideas through the empty traditions of human beings and the empty superstitions of spirit beings. But that's not the way of Christ. Everything of God gets expressed in him, so you can see and hear him clearly.

The power of the Gospel is demonstrated not in our programs or lectures, but in a transformed life living freely in the world. We are the sermon the world needs, and the sermon that can help others grow to know him. It's our living in him that makes the difference, not just talking about him.

. . . .

CHAPTER 16

THE CONVERSATIONS THAT MATTER MOST

Over thirty-five years ago, I was with a group of pastors discussing where we felt most alive in "the ministry." It didn't take long for me to answer. It came in those moments when I stood on the edge of a stage, Bible in hand, expounding some Scripture with my voice raised, more words in my mouth than I could get out in a reasonable amount of time. It was thrilling to hold the crowd in the palm of my hand as they hung on every word, either laughing uproariously or moved to tears by some insight I was sharing.

But I was only in my mid-twenties at the time, so hopefully my ignorance can be excused. I wouldn't give the same answer today. As I look back, I now know how deeply that moment appealed to my own needs more than it served those listening to me. Now I find my greatest joy opening a door for someone to see into a bigger reality and watching the lights come on in their heart.

I've preached from massive stages, and I've sat in living rooms conversing with a few dozen people. Most people drawn into "ministry" seek the stage—the larger the crowd, the better. That's how we've measured success and, quite honestly, it is much easier to deliver a preplanned sermon than to ride the ups and downs of a free-flowing conversation with its unforeseen course changes and difficult questions.

However, if you were going to be with someone you wanted to learn from, where would you rather be—part of a large audience or having a conversation over a meal? If I were invited to a golf lesson from a famous golf pro, I would much prefer he and I alone on a driving range than being in a stadium watching him on a JumboTron. And how different the lesson would be! From the stage, he'd talk in generalities, and everyone would have to try the same technique hours later when they got to a golf course and no longer remember the lesson. If it were just the two of us, he could look at my swing, listen to the problems I'm having, and offer me solutions I could immediately try.

Over the past forty years, I've watched a lovely shift in my thinking about teaching and helping others on this journey. I've gone from thinking success and efficiency are found where I address a macro audience—a number of people I don't know through sermons, podcasting, or publishing—to knowing that the most transformative moments come in conversations with people I'm getting to know.

As I've traveled over the last twenty years, I've been particularly aware that the smaller and more interactive the conversations were, the more enduring fruit they produced. I now know that the engagements that happen before and after the meetings have the most impact on others. Riding in a car, sitting down to a meal, or just pausing to answer an individual question all have more impact. That's why I prefer to stay in homes, not hotels, and prefer conversations to speaking engagements.

As I read the Gospels now, it is easy to see that Jesus spent a lot more time in personal engagements than he did lecturing crowds. He talked with the Pharisees; he didn't debate them. He was in their homes as well as those of his friends. He found a boat trip across Galilee as propitious a place to share the reality of the kingdom as he did sitting beside a well in Samaria. He sought out Zaccheus for lunch when a large crowd was seeking his attention on the street.

Before you point out that Jesus also spoke to large crowds, I'm well aware of that. I am not suggesting that they are evil, only that they aren't the most effective way to help people embrace the life of his Father. It has caused me to think a lot about what I do in macro or micro engagements. Macro engagements include speaking to groups, publishing books or website content, or producing podcasts or other recordings. I do a lot of that because I enjoy it and feel called to put some information in the world that way. So, I'm not against it; I just realize how limited it is.

Though Jesus spoke to crowds, he didn't seek them or gather them. He didn't organize and promote any meeting; they found him. Even then, many in the crowds left confused and unengaged. It was the extra time he spent with his disciples and others that helped them get what they had missed earlier. The most formative moments in my journey have not come from lectures but from personal engagements.

I'm not saying large crowds are evil and small crowds are good. This isn't an either-or discussion. We can make room for both, even as we recognize that the reality of Jesus' life passes on better in table-sized conversations than in large-scale meetings. What's bothering me is that so many people, especially those who aspire to ministry, pursue the macro engagements in speaking and publishing, spending more time trying to build an audience of strangers than grow in conversations with people they already know. So many are worried about expanding their influence, building their platform, fighting for speaking engagements, and pushing their books or podcasts hoping to gain traction as an expert, when the greatest opportunities to share the kingdom live in the relationships they already have. Everyone gets to participate there, not just gifted writers or eloquent speakers.

And unless our space in the macro world doesn't grow out of our lives at a personal level, it can easily create an environment where the realities of the kingdom are easily distorted. The lure to have influence gratifies our ego, if not our pocketbook. Dazzled by the lights and popularity of the stage, many buy into the false notion that those who occupy it are significant people and their words reflect God's heart. But do they really?

I'm not convinced. The macro conversation values the wrong realities—the youthful entertainer over the wise sage, the energetic entrepreneur over the servant, and the manipulation of crowd dynamics over the integrity of open and honest dialog. It prizes the well-crafted illusion instead of the integrity of the speaker. Audiences really don't know the person in front of them, only the illusion they want to create, and there may be little connection between them.

We need to look no further than the allegations against Bill Cosby, who lived for decades as an admired man on the stage for his humor and insight, and yet seems to have used that notoriety to exploit women who sought his help. The fact that we don't know tells you everything we need to know about the stage and how little we know about the person on it. I met one popular Christian author who was sleeping with his girlfriend while he was going through a divorce. I asked him if he had any conflicts between his writings and his current lifestyle. "Oh, you think I'm trying to live what I write?" he asked, as if I was from another planet. "I'm not. I'm a writer to a Christian marketplace. This is how I make my living; I know how to write what they want to hear."

How many times have you been disappointed to discover a person's public persona was at odds with their private life? Anne Lamott wrote, "The most degraded and sometimes nearly evil men I have known were all writers who'd had bestsellers." The most nonrelational people I've ever met have written books on relationships. Watching how someone treats their spouse, their staff, and others around them will tell you far more about them than anything they share on a stage.

Not everyone on the stage is a fraud; there are some who offer a genuine and compassionate voice, but they are few. The pursuit of the stage twists something in us, putting self-promotion above people, and most become a caricature, perfecting cute slogans and three easy steps that never work, instead of a genuine person. To hold on to it you have to perpetuate the illusion and manipulate people around you. That's why people on a stage act differently than anyone in real life, with the tones they use and the demeanor they display. They live in illusions, creating fake communities to appeal to the need to belong, offer "special" wisdom and insight to put them above others, and convince people they've never met that they love and care about them.

Meanwhile people of profound wisdom live right down the

street from us untapped. The men and women I've met on this journey who are the most Christlike and have impacted me the most don't live on a stage or have a website. They are content to know their love for others, and engagements with them are far more fruitful. So, we must use the macro world advisedly. It is not evil, it just lends itself to honoring the wrong realities. Celebrity culture disfigures almost everyone who touches it. It is easier to be perceived as an expert on a stage than live as a brother or sister on a journey. It allows you to pontificate unchallenged, and say things to people you wouldn't have the courage to address face-to-face. How many sermons have you heard that were thinly veiled admonishments to someone who had offended the speaker? I've done it, too, to my regret, but it's a coward's way out.

I wouldn't discourage you from putting your voice out there, however God gives you opportunity. I do all those things because I know it can help people I'll never meet, but at the same time I know that those things are not the most significant things I do. Perhaps they should take about the same priority in our lives that we see in the gospel, about 80 percent of our time in the micro conversations that matter, and only 20 percent to faceless audiences as a way to plant seeds. And that 20 percent is best when the crowd is organic and wanting to seek our help, not when it has been contrived through self-promotion.

Let's value our personal engagements more highly. This has not been a philosophical shift for me; it was an experiential one first. I began to notice where the kingdom really thrives, and it is rarely on a stage. That environment is too one-dimensional, offering principles in a one-size-fits-all format, rather than helping someone make a next step in their journey. On a recent flight home, I ended up in a conversation with a broken man that was far more powerful than any other conversation or presentation I had on the trip.

It reminds me again that God really rescues one sheep at a time, and the real power of his kingdom comes in personal engagements and growing friendships rather than events, outreaches, or meetings. So look for the next conversation Jesus has for you—with an old friend on the phone, a stranger in line at the market, or a neighbor across the fence. Nothing else offers more opportunity for people to engage God's reality.

Those I've met who are giving up on our institutions aren't looking for a more engaging sermon, but a different environment where people learn through dialog, where they are not pressed for conformity of thought, but are free to explore their own transformation. This doesn't minimize the gifts of teaching and encouragement, but reframes them in a different and far more challenging environment, where the quality of someone's character is more important than their ability to turn a phrase.

Of course, the elephant in the living room we haven't discussed yet is the business model that underlies these two conversations. It is easy to monetize the macro conversation. Our culture is set up for that. But it is impossible to monetize the micro conversation, and for those who seek to make their living by the Gospel, that is a problem. Or is it? We'll look at that in the next chapter.

CHAPTER 17

. . . .

THE PITFALLS OF MONETIZING MINISTRY

"Follow the Money!"

Since Watergate, it has been the prevailing wisdom to ferret out excess and corruption in our treasured institutions. There is something about money, especially in huge amounts, that causes people to justify compromising their integrity by making personal gain more important than the Father's purposes.

As an increasing number of people grow disillusioned with the abuse and excesses of our religious institutions, many also have a growing awareness that those same institutions have strayed from the purity and simplicity of devotion to Christ. Perhaps they need to look no further than how money and high finance has corrupted the authenticity of the Gospel. When someone, or an institution, makes their livelihood from the things of God, it is so easy to be seduced into serving their bottom line, even at the expense of the Gospel.

And while I'm not suggesting it is wrong for people to make their living from their ministry, I don't think we are critical enough in assessing how often the best economic choices are at odds with how God works. Thus, we end up distorting the Gospel, even as we claim to follow it. Why have we committed the vitality of his kingdom to the same business models used by every other human enterprise in the world, and what are the consequences of doing so?

Isn't that why we have ended up with a plethora of religious institutions that are more often preoccupied with their own power and security than they are demonstrating Christ's love in the world? Some would argue that the religious industry we created is just a natural extension of the things Jesus taught, and the way to get his message in the world. However, the excesses and distortions of our institutions say otherwise, and many have grown unchecked for centuries. Is it just coincidence that our large institutions pay exorbitant salaries to those at the top, or can justify harming others to protect themselves and their organization?

In the previous chapter, I asserted that the reason we have more large-scale meetings about the life of Jesus, when personal conversations can be far more fruitful, is because we don't have a business model that undergirds more personal connections. We have an industry for teachers and writers that rewards those who are successful at leveraging the marketplace for money and influence, and in such environments the message of Christ suffers.

Jesus warned us that the reality of his kingdom would not mix well with the human thirst for money and power. The ability for any of us to believe something just because it is in our self-interest is well documented in psychological testing. I'm not talking here about people who deceive others for money, but about our ability to convince ourselves something is true that isn't, so long as we profit enough for doing so. And the more money involved, the easier it is to deceive ourselves and others around us. It's called cognitive dissonance, where we justify what we know is wrong because we feel as if we have to.

I used to teach tithing as a New Testament mandate. I grew up with that conviction and had no problem making that conclusion from Scripture when my salary was drawn from those to whom I taught it. Only when my income was no longer attached to other people's tithes could I begin to see that God's purpose in the new covenant was not the obligation of tithing, but joy of generosity that would spill out of our hearts. Tithing is a cheap substitute in that light.

Monetizing anything changes the nature of it. I've watched the apps on my smartphone or websites I frequent all become worse when the goal is to monetize it rather than provide the service for which it was originally intended. Who even remembers Facebook when it was just information about your friends, rather than an endless string of advertisements and political posturing? Nothing is made better by monetizing it; in fact, it often becomes twisted by benefiting the provider more than the one it was meant to serve. Nowhere is that truer than the Gospel.

CHAPTER 18

. . . .

THE GOSPEL AS A GIFT

When Lewis Hyde wrote about Alcoholics Anonymous (AA) in his classic book on creativity, *The Gift*, he pointed to one of its characteristics that has assured not only its effectiveness but also its longevity: participating in AA is free, and it always has been. Nothing is bought or sold; no one makes his living from facilitating its meetings. Hyde wrote, "Local groups are autonomous and meet their minimal expenses—coffee, literature—through member contributions. Those grateful for the impact it has had on their lives, volunteer their time to help others."

Hyde concluded, "AA probably wouldn't be as effective, in fact, if the program was delivered through the machinery of the market, not because its lessons would have to change, but because the spirit behind them would be different." He asserts that the gift may be the actual agent of change, and that selling a transformative gift falsifies the relationship between the two parties.

Do you hear Jesus' words, "Freely you have received, freely give," running through your mind? I do. What would the church of Jesus Christ be like today if it had followed AA's model of generosity and volunteerism instead of McDonald's model of franchise marketing? Even AA's approach has been corrupted when congregations make it part of their ministry with a staff position and a line item in the budget. Though it starts out having a profound impact on lives, it often ends up an object of conflict and competition, and becomes unsustainable.

Part of the reason we have so many different religious institutions has to do with contest for money and power. The larger they grow, the more demand there is to protect and provide for the machinery. Jealousies and power struggles are the natural result, and the disaffected go off to start their own. We prove we're businesses when we labor under the ultimatums of large donors, or force departing pastors to sign noncompete clauses to get their severance pay. Once someone has to be paid a salary, or buildings have to be provided, the decision-making revolves around economics, and nothing distorts the life of Jesus more quickly than the business model, flow charts, and the insatiable need for money. It is no longer a gift; it's a big business with many depending on its sustenance and growth. Our entire religious system is built that way, from seminaries to churches and publishers.

Jesus said it was impossible to serve God and money. We think we can blend them without consequence, but money always wins out, even among those who start out with the purest ideals. Money blinds us to the ways God works, and the need for it pressures us in ways no one likes. I know pastors who walk on eggshells each week, knowing they can't honestly share their journey and not run into trouble with some faction in the church. I worked with a publisher that wanted me to change the content of *He Loves Me* so pastors would be more inclined to read it from their pulpits and an editor who wouldn't print an article I'd written even though he loved it. What if it offended the subscriber base and they cancelled their subscriptions? They all know that even a decline of a few percentage points in offerings or subscribers can mean the difference between staying in *business* or not.

I know that's hard to see from the inside. Everyone thinks they are doing God's will as best they know how, rarely considering how much their need for income shapes that. I've told many a pastor who is critical of those who are done with their congregation, "If you could just step away from all of this for two years, you would be shocked at the things you'd discover when money no longer influences your ministry." I had no idea how much the economic religious systems we've created blurred my vision, until I found myself no longer dependent on it.

In short, we get the Gospel we pay for, or click on, and the cost of that is losing the simplicity and power of the life of Jesus once delivered to the saints. It has to be complicated so people can sell their books or seminars. I heard one man say recently to a group of ministers wanting to enhance their income to take their best teaching and craft it into a set of principles. "If you can systematize it, you can monetize it." Yes, he pinged my yuck meter, but it does explain why we have more five-point plans than we have people ready to equip others to follow Jesus.

Most ministries begin with the question of what has to be done to finance it. From the start, money becomes the overriding consideration, rather than the content of the message they hope to convey. Most conscientious pastors I know would love to be independently wealthy and not be controlled by the boards and expectations of others. They recognize how much it encroaches on their liberty and influences their decisions.

It's not that money is intrinsically evil; it's that our desire for it is inherently deceptive.

CHAPTER 19

. . . .

"FULL-TIME MINISTRY"

Yet "full-time" Christian ministry is the dream of so many people, and that exists now almost exclusively inside a religious marketplace that generates hundreds of millions of dollars in sales and donations. For some, they just hope to find a vocation in the religious industry, either to work around Christians or in hopes of finding purpose and meaning. What many don't realize is how much time you'll spend managing people, fundraising, and program planning to keep the machinery running, and how complicated it can be when other egos get involved.

Not all of this is bad, of course. While some of it genuinely supports God's work in the world, much more of it works against him. Many Christian publishers are now publicly traded corporations, whose only purpose is to maximize profits for the shareholders. Others just trade in religious content to carve out a lucrative lifestyle. Is it any surprise that our religious industries function exactly like their worldly counterparts valuing the same things they do—size, influence, money, and notoriety? When that happens, you can be sure that we've moved from the kingdom of God to a kingdom of our own making. Jesus told us, "What people value highly is detestable in God's sight" (Luke 16:15). We may still be talking about his kingdom, but we've long since ceased to serve it. His kingdom values obscurity over notoriety, serving others over being served, small and flexible over large and rigid, and following his leading whatever it risks, instead of making the best business decision.

How we navigate that space discerningly is critical to the future of God's purpose in the world. For most, these words will hold no more impact than spitting into gale-force winds, but I'm writing primarily for those who want to be a voice for God in the world, not those who simply want to make their living in the religious trade. I realize there are many writers, artists, pastors, and teachers who prefer to make their living in this industry and aren't too worried about the larger issue as to how their institution expresses God's character in the world.

I'm not arguing that all publishing is evil or that selling a book or that all advertising on a website of itself dishonors the kingdom. This is a heavily nuanced consideration, and one that I continue to wrestle with. I have worked for religious organizations, owned a publishing company, and sold a lot of my own books, all of which helped provide for my family. That said, there can be great value in freeing up the time of more mature brothers and sisters to help others find their growth and freedom in Christ. That can be a great blessing, even though the pitfalls are enormous, and we don't have the best track record over the last 2,000 years proving any of us can resist those temptations.

Maybe Watchman Nee had it right in *The Normal Christian Church Life* when he offered a different way of thinking for those who make their living by the Gospel: "Every worker, no matter what his ministry, must exercise faith for the meeting of all his personal needs and all the needs of his work. In God's Word (sic) we read of no worker asking for, or receiving, a salary for his services. That God's servants should look to human sources for the supply of their needs has no precedent in Scripture. No servant of God should look to any human agency, whether an individual or a society, for the meeting of his temporal needs. If they can be met by the labor of his own hands or from a private income, well and good. Otherwise he should be directly dependent on God alone for their supply, as were the early apostles. ...If a man can trust God, let him go and work for Him. If not, let him stay at home, for he lacks the first qualification for the work."

The first time I read that I felt sick. It's what I'd always feared was true. Who could live that way? It was the stuff of Rees Howells, not Wayne Jacobsen. In the intervening years, however, I've been convinced otherwise. We were not given a message of love to turn it into an income stream. The Gospel was never meant to be someone's source of living; it was meant to set a world free into the love of a Gracious Father.

It's one thing to make a life or teaching available and live off the generosity that might come from that, and another thing to monetize the ministry, distort the Scriptures wittingly or unwittingly, and exploit people with guilt to increase the money flow. It's less about where the money comes from than it is the dangers of distorting the Gospel when our livelihood is at stake. If our dependence is on him, there will be no reason to distort the message for personal gain, even if some of the mechanism includes book sales.

I have no problem with people deriving income from their craft, whether it is carpentry, car sales, writing, or teaching. This is not an argument against people being in full-time ministry. It is the consideration that when we seek to use the Gospel as our income stream we will inevitably distort it. You'll know them because maximizing sales is their goal, not helping others find their life and freedom in Jesus. Some can work inside that system as God gives opportunity, but won't sell out to their ambitions.

It's not an easy road to walk and I have plenty of regrets about past decisions I've made, but the more I've learned to trust Father for my resources and simply put things in the world to bless others, the easier it has been to follow my conscience and not financial expedience. Though I sell books, I also give them away and have free resources on my website to help others. I travel at my own expense and do not charge a fee for speaking. I've come to rely on God's generosity and it has made all the difference.

CHAPTER 20

. . . .

IT'S NOT ABOUT CHANGING THE SYSTEM, IT'S LETTING GOD CHANGE YOU

Will a book like this change our vast religious industry even a little bit? Of course not, and that's not why I'm writing it. I hope, however, it makes you wiser as you engage the religious marketplace, and encourage those who pay a difficult price to put the purity of the Gospel above their own personal expedience.

When something in the religious marketplace doesn't seem right to you, look to the financial demands behind it and sniff out whether it is influencing what is being said or done. How do you know? If it breeds an ongoing dependency on the person behind it, if the website is more about building a personal kingdom than God's, or if it offers formulas and principles instead of a real relationship with Christ, it's driven by someone needing to make a living. They are really not that hard to spot when the website is so filled with ads it looks like a race car, or if it promises something for free, but only in exchange for your email address. There's a generosity inside God's working that will prevent people from using the same conventions the world does to build its business.

Recognize the difference between a gifted man or woman putting light and life into the world, and those who are wrapped up in the machinery of the marketplace and are constantly trying to exploit their audience to maximize their income through sales, website clicks, or charging exorbitant fees for conferences or seminars. Does it look like they are maximizing their exposure and income, or genuinely looking for ways to build up others? Do they fall into the industry trap of producing a new book every year that doesn't bring anything new to the table? Do they easily move between the "church world" and the business world, offering the same marketing wisdom to sell books, build your platform, or brand your message? Holding workshops with their unique terminology, so they can train others to do it exactly the way they do it, is a sure sign that someone is building their own empire rather than letting Jesus build his kingdom.

You can tell money has trapped you in ministry if you don't have the freedom to follow your heart without risking your income. I know many pastors who stay in ministry, admitting they are making the best of a bad situation because they don't think they are employable outside of it. If your need is to make a living or pay bills, you will make an entirely different set of decisions than if you didn't have to worry about money at all, knowing God would take care of you. The world puts more of a premium on the job skills of those who've been in ministry than the individual himself. Those who have led volunteer organizations, managed budgets, trained others, and can act responsibly are valuable assets in the business world. I've seen many former pastors go on to fruitful careers and more time for real ministry with others than they did hassling with the politics of a religious institution. Don't just bury your head and go along for fear God can't take care of you. Find what he really has for you, and as you blossom in it, you'll also find ministry more a joy when it is a gift than a means of income.

For those who want to share their gifts with the body of Christ beyond their personal connections, separate the gift from your income stream, or else the lust for influence and security will shape the message in ways you won't recognize. Let God teach you how he wants to be your provider, whether that's by some tentmaking enterprise as Paul did, or employment that leaves you some free time to help others.

If you can trust God to provide for you as you make yourself available to others, do so. The proof will be in his provision. I've seen many go down that road to bankruptcy in presumption of a calling God had not given them. If you go into debt to follow him, he's not the one leading you. That doesn't mean you have to give everything away. I think a writer is worth his book sales, or a teacher worth his expenses; just make sure you're not manipulating people to get what you want.

If you've ever watched someone switch from offering their insights as a gift, to monetizing it every way they can, it is not a pretty sight and their message gets twisted. You can seek popularity or you can trade in truth, but the two don't go hand-in-hand. Some even boast of making six figures from advertising on their ministry website as they spend time teaching others how to do it. In doing so, however, they become less a gift to the body of Christ. For most, it doesn't work anyway. It is not easy to make a living from your creative gifts, whether they are in writing, speaking, video, music, or acting. The creative arts reward a select few obscenely and the rest meagerly. Everyone with a creative bent would love to make it their vocation rather than a hobby, but only a very few find enough opportunity to do that. Make it your labor of love and let it grow organically, rather than through false promotion and manipulation. If it generates enough opportunity and income to free up your time, be grateful to God, but in the long run it isn't your choice.

If you want to engage in ministry, don't look for things to do to pay the bills. Do what you do because God asks you, and watch him provide in ways you can't even imagine. If you are more excited about helping others than being known, there is plenty of opportunity already around you. There is so much you can freely give away if you don't have to worry about being compensated for it.

Let generosity grow. In time, those who've been touched by your life may want to help support you to share that same benefit with others. To me, this is the best kind of giving, not from the people I'm with at the moment, but from others I've touched in the past who want to help me touch others in the world. At financially critical times in my past, we'd receive money from someone completely unsolicited who said they'd been touched by something I'd said or written and wanted to help us be able to share it with others. It's amazing how God provides that way just at the right time and without us having to make our need known. It's a great way for people to help put the kingdom into the world.

When you find those who are gifted at helping others to live deeply in the life of Jesus, and if they live a life that backs it up, look for ways to support them. And don't think I'm writing this for some hidden need in my life. I honestly don't need it, but it is a powerful way to help put conversations that matter into the world, without having to create ministries and churches that have expensive infrastructure and priorities other than participating in Jesus' kingdom.

The freedom to give his life away is the heart of real ministry. Admittedly, embracing that freedom is not easy and is a long process. Thinking I'm living by faith without knowing him or following his desires is merely presumption. Real trust only grows inside a relationship based on love. As it does, especially with our provision, we can live more freely from the demands of money that will inevitably shape us in the world's image.

I was in vocational ministry from the moment I left college. It wasn't until I was forty-two that I had someone simply ask if they could get my help, without them feeling as if I was getting paid to give it to them. The difference in that encounter from the thousands of appointments I had done previously was palpable, and its fruitfulness was far greater than anything I had known. When he left, his gratitude was effusive because he had received it as a gift, not an expectation on my time. That made the impact of our conversation all the greater. That moment started me down a different road than I'd known before. Serving others is a gift. There is no way to monetize it without tainting it, so give his life away and watch how his generosity will care for you.

Then you will no longer have to follow the money. You'll be free instead to follow the Lamb wherever he goes.

CHAPTER 21

. . . .

WAITING FOR REVIVAL...

I hear it everywhere I go.

"I believe we're on the verge of a great revival." People say it with that faraway look in their eyes as they gaze off into the spiritual ether.

I have no reason to doubt their sincerity or their hopes, for I used to be one of them. As a pastor of a local congregation I knew that something was amiss. While some amazing things happened in our fellowship over the years, there was an unsettling undercurrent that tore at my heart: the ridiculous expectations, the burdensome program, the political bickering, and the soul-numbing routine that was not often as life-giving as I'd hoped. To add wisdom to injury, every time I would read the Gospels I was reminded that Jesus never got caught up in those things.

And I've been hearing people pine away for this coming revival for over fifty years. It's the same people, too, who keep telling themselves it's just "right around the corner." Regardless of how you feel about Pensacola, Toronto, or Redding, none of them grew beyond their own borders or the celebrities they spawned, nor did they move beyond the kind of miraculous encounters that are easily replicated by group dynamics and the power of suggestion. That's not to say that God didn't touch people in some marvelous ways, but none of these proved to be the widespread revival folks have hoped for.

When I try to pin people down to what that revival looks like, most hark back to the Welsh revival, Charles Finney, or even the Jesus People days of the early '70s. They describe people being overwhelmed with conviction and coming to the Lord in repentance, or an outpouring of supernatural power that draws the media and swells attendance at local congregations. In all cases they paint the image of a stadium-sized crowd caught up in an ecstatic experience. Almost no one describes what it would look like in the world.

My more cerebral colleagues wait less for some kind of supernatural encounter, but they do hope a new structure will emerge from the current dissatisfaction that will make the church more relevant in this century, without compromising the authenticity of the Gospel once delivered to the saints. Every year a new onslaught of books promises to offer new structures that will carry the church further in the twenty-first century, but in time they all fade away to be replaced by a new set of books offering yet more possibilities.

Perhaps nothing exposes the emptiness of our religious pursuits more than waiting for this revival, or the endless search for a better structure. Underneath both is the tacit admission that what we currently see falls short of what we hunger to experience. We want an active God, overrunning the culture with the coming kingdom, just as Jesus did with a Gospel that engages people and transforms them in a way the world cannot ignore. What does that search say except that God isn't already at work to engage this world and unfold his kingdom among us?

If you think God has stopped doing those things and is waiting capriciously for some future date to finally give us all the good stuff, then you may want to reconsider. What kind of God would that be? Jesus already told us that his Father is *always* working. Could it be true that while we're waiting for the revival we seek, we miss what he's already doing around us?

That turned out to be true for me. In my days of waiting for something incredible that would infuse our congregation with a fresh dose of passion and power, I only grew increasingly frustrated. Our endless prayer meetings seemed to make no difference. I begged him and he seemed silent. It wasn't until years later that I discovered he hadn't been silent after all. He'd been nudging me down a road I couldn't see because I was so focused on him doing what I thought best.

But I only discovered that after I found myself excluded from the congregation I had helped to plant, due to a contest of power I didn't have the heart to engage. Though I was offered numerous pastoral jobs elsewhere, I was not interested. I figured I would find my way back into another congregation at some point, but I wasn't in a hurry to do so. I wanted to decompress. During that time, my wife and I began to discover that the renewal we had hoped for was already happening beyond the walls of our traditional congregation.

We saw God at work in people around us, and began to taste of the worldwide phenomenon of people who were all spontaneously and simultaneously moving beyond the traditional congregational to learn to live in the Father's affection and freely share it with others. It captured our hearts and allowed us to embrace a depth of community with others that wasn't distracted by structures and programs. It's made me wonder that we don't see it encased in a building or a conference anywhere because the moment it is, it begins to wither under human control. Honestly, I couldn't have seen it as long as I was focused on the religious system we had built and prayed so hard for God to revitalize.

I know that's threatening to those who think the only place God can move is in a sanctioned institution, but that is only because they haven't looked elsewhere. I was shocked by the people I met outside those structures who were passionate about following Jesus, loving others, and sharing his life with the world around them. I often tell people who are so condemning of people outside that they have no idea what they would see of God's reality if they set aside all their institutional engagements for two years. It takes some time for the fog to clear, but many discover that God was at work in many ways they just couldn't see when they were focused on the endless activities, political wrangling, and corporate needs of an institution.

Even people leaving may be part of the very revival those who condemn them are praying for. Some have tagged them the "Dones," but what many of them are craving is a simpler, more authentic faith that becomes part of the fabric of their daily lives. It's the routine and obligations of an institution that lull many to spiritual slumber.

The reason I no longer pray for revival is because I'm already living in the reality I hoped it would bring. The reason I don't seek a new church model is because I discovered that it wasn't important. God moves among people, not systems, and while he can move in and around any system we devise, it is not his priority to revive systems, but to renew people.

That's already going on around you and if you miss it, it's because your eyes aren't focused on what he is doing, but on what you want to see him do. Jesus warned us that those who sought miraculous signs would most likely miss them when they came, because they don't come the way we think they should or in the places we want to see them. Maybe it's not what's happening down at the altar under the bright TV lights that matters, but in the woman sitting in the balcony crying by herself. Perhaps it isn't in the conference or revival service, but in a coworker you've never even had the courage to get to know, a neighbor who hides behind their front door, or the person sitting next to you on the train.

Jesus didn't share our preoccupation with large-scale revivals or even crafting more relevant structures. While he did miracles and healed the sick, he didn't use them to start a movement or draw the crowd. In fact, he downplayed them more than not because his compassion was directed at people, not visibility. Even Jesus' brothers questioned why he did these things in Galilee rather than going to Jerusalem and becoming a public figure.

Perhaps Jesus explained it best when he talked about leaving the ninety-nine sheep to go seek the one that was lost. That's where the Shepherd works, not with ninety-nine who think themselves secure, but with the one who knows they are lost. His larger point just may have been that ministry happens best one at a time. That is why he told us to "Love one another," not to "Love everyone." Love is best applied in the singular, the next person in front of you, rather than trying to draw a crowd or change the culture.

While Jesus taught crowds on occasion, his most compelling moments came on boat trips with his disciples, spending an afternoon with a woman at a well in Samaria, or having lunch with Zaccheus when the streets were lined with people who wanted to see the miracle-worker from Galilee. Something gets distorted in crowds that makes it more difficult for us to see what God is doing. We are easily distracted by fame and by the identity that a crowd brings, while God is more interested in the heart.

That's why I scratch my head now when I see people who are willing to fly around the world to pray for a revival, when they wouldn't walk across the street, or even across the aisle, on a Sunday morning to engage someone desperately in need of love. We'd rather go to a strategy meeting to reach the lost than strike up a conversation with a person we're sitting next to on the plane. We are so busy seeking the crowd, the large-scale, attention-grabbing events, that we miss the way Jesus works behind the scenes to touch people every day. The more I get involved in the needs and struggles of individuals, the more I see how he intervenes and rescues people in incredible ways. Isn't this how he asked us to love?

Almost daily I hear of some amazing things God is doing to share his love with people. I am excited by the way he draws people into his life and addresses their deepest needs with his power. That's why when I hear people pining away for a future revival, I want to shake them and say, "Don't you see what is already happening around you?" God is alive and moving in the world in ways that astound me nearly every day.

This quest for revival is a focus on the ninety-nine, and not on the one. Revivals begin with the people to love, not with outpourings or structure changes. It's not programs that need reformation, but enough people to embrace the perspective that loving "one another" is the currency of this kingdom. Whether we gather in buildings or not, it is the loving that will change the world, and it can only happen one life at a time. Revivals aren't contrived by prayer rallies, celebrity leaders, or human programs; they merely result from people discovering and sharing God's love as freely as he shares it with them.

Whatever revival we see in the coming years won't be the result of a long-awaited divine intervention. Remember he is always working, and that includes today. Rather than praying for a revival or a better way to do church, we might just ask him to show us what he is already doing around us, and participate with him there. Who is he giving you to love today? How does he want to touch that life and how is he asking you to care for them?

If any larger-scale revival is in the wings, this is where it will begin anyway.

CHAPTER 22

· · · · · · · · · · · · ·

A HEART FOR
WHAT'S TRUE

When did truth become more important than love?

When I grew up in Christianity, I was taught that you had to believe the truth to be saved. Of course, loving each other was encouraged, but certainly not with the same passion. So, living to doctrine and defending it when challenged were more important than loving others, even though Jesus specifically told us to do the latter. In fact, he said our capacity to love would win the world, not our eloquence with the truth.

Truth without love more often destroys people than helps them. Those who explore theology alone, and don't mine the depths of God's love and character, can't help but be a bit obnoxious. For them, it is all about believing the right thing, and what they miss is a process of transformation. They are often angry, manipulative, and judgmental. On what basis, then, has truth set them free? Are they gentler, more loving, and kinder to others who are lost? In my experience? No.

That may be why Jesus and Paul both told us love was more important, because they knew that without love, people would not be able to discover truth. I'm convinced that truth does not travel well outside of love. You speak the truth without it, and little good it does. But real love will never ignore the truth. Love always seeks what's true and then graciously draws people toward that light. When we appreciate that love is the most important part of truth and the environment in which people are freest to discover it, we never need to choose love at the expense of truth.

Unfortunately, however, for two thousand years Christians have staked their identity on being right. Battles over doctrine, even down to insignificant minutiae, have divided us into innumerable factions, each one believing they have more truth than the others. So that instead of learning to love each other beyond our differences, every difference is a test of who is right and who is wrong. We get sucked into the same game the world plays of having to convince those who disagree with us of how wrong they are.

I see the fallout from that every day in my Facebook feed, especially as people try to convince their friends that the truth they see is the truth everyone needs to believe. And the more insecure someone is, the more they are drawn into the battle over truth instead of learning how to love. We expend far more energy trying to prove someone wrong than we do helping them discover how loved they are.

We often do it without thinking. Recently I asked for some input on a book cover design. I got over 300 responses, and the majority registered their preference as if it was the only right option. People who didn't see it the same way were wrong, not just seeing it differently. When we no longer separate preference from fact, we express ourselves in a way that is off-putting to others, and it closes more doors than it opens.

Nowhere is this more evident today than in the argument about whether or not someone must go to a local congregation to be a Christian. Everyone fights for their point of view, convinced that anyone who disagrees with them is wrong. One seeks validation of their faith experience, the other demands compliance, and both divide the body of Christ not on the basis of Truth, but on personal preference.

Much of the angst I've seen in those "done" with religious institutions is the need to convince those who meet in those systems that what they are doing is wrong and hurtful, or those inside try to convince those outside that they can't be part of Jesus' church without attending a local institution. As I've observed over the years, some of those who most ardently defended local congregations when they were leading them are the most damning now that they are on the outside.

If you live by right or wrong alone, you will inevitably condemn others to validate yourself. A lot of that dialog stems from insecurity—people who need the affirmation of others to validate their own conclusions. Both misunderstand the nature of truth and how God wins us into it. Of course, this conflict is exacerbated by social media platforms because arrogant, polarizing commentary generates more response than grace-filled commentary does. We care more about being right on an issue than we do about being right with each other.

"Truth cannot be compromised" is the motto of both sides of any conflict, and while true enough on the face of it, it doesn't recognize how much of what we fight for is not truth itself, but only our view of it. How often have you ardently defended something you found out later was based on misunderstanding or misinformation? One of the joys of this journey is discovering that God's wisdom far exceeds ours on everything, and we are constantly growing to understand what's true and what is only fabrications of our desires. That's why Jesus wanted us to know that truth was not the perfect alignment of our doctrinal ducks, but our connection to a Person who is Truth itself. By believing him we believe in all truth, even the parts we don't know yet.

That's why one of the telltale signs of someone growing in truth is humility. Knowing they see dimly into God's reality allows them to hold it lightly and not seek to force it on others.

Their tone expresses that this is the best they see it today, not this is the only way a real child of God can see it. When you hear that kind of arrogance, back away. This is someone who knows doctrine better than they know God. Find those who can discuss differences of opinion graciously, knowing that love, not judgment, is the best way to help people discover truth, and that growing in truth has more to do with learning to depend on him than amassing intellectual knowledge alone.

None of this is to say, of course, that truth is not important, only that most of our truth isn't truth with a capital T, but simply our own conclusions based on the comfort it gives us at the time. I'm all for getting our theology straight; I'm not a relativist. I don't believe everyone gets to decide what's true. What's true in the universe is how God designed it to work and created us to live in it. Where we embrace that reality, we get to live freely, even in a broken world not immune from its pain, but also not overwhelmed by it. There are only a precious few big-ticket items that provide the basis of life in Christ, and none of them are essential to be loved because love opens the door to truth.

One of Jesus' most oft-quoted statements is "You will know the truth, and the truth will set you free" (John 8:32). Mostly those words are misapplied as if he's referring to the right set of beliefs, and are used to justify people forcing their point of view on others. What if, however, he was not only telling us what truth could do, but how to share it with others? It is valuable when it sets people free, and disastrous when it seeks to manipulate people to do what we think best.

The ways of the world are all built on lies—about God, about ourselves, about success and failure, about what we value and how we engage others. Believe the lies and you become imprisoned by them in a long, slow death spiral. Truth is the bright light that penetrates the darkness. Our initial tendency is not to run to it, but to shield our eyes and stay in the false comfort of those lies. Love is what makes the light inviting instead of repelling.

When I read the Gospels, I am increasingly aware of how careful Jesus was with the truth. The truth is powerful stuff. It can blow up someone's entire world. That's a great thing when they are ready for it, but it can be horribly destructive if they are not. That's why he was so mindful how, when, and with whom he shared truth. He sometimes couched it in stories so people who weren't ready to receive it wouldn't understand it.

If you've ever tried to convince someone that something is true when they don't want to hear it, you know how impossible it is. When Jesus spoke clearly, he was talking to those who were curious. Even then he didn't talk about truth as a set of theological concepts to believe, but the truth that allows you to see past the lies that ensnare us and sets you free to embrace God's reality. The only time he confronted people with truth they weren't ready for was when their actions were doing great damage to others, and even then he wasn't heard. There's nothing more glorious than truth that brings freedom and nothing more destructive than beating others up with truth we think they should hear.

Fifteen years ago, I was riding in a car with my dad when he asked me a question: "Do you enjoy what you're doing now?" Five years earlier I had been a pastor of a growing congregation in the central part of California. Through a painful set of circumstances I got separated from that group, and he wasn't sure how content I was with the consulting, writing, and traveling. I thought he was really asking if I missed being a pastor.

I thought about it for a moment and realized that I had moved from being a leader of a conformity-based system to a brother alongside people seeking to find their freedom in Christ. "Well, Dad I used to walk around with a set of keys making sure everyone was locked into their cells. For the past five years I've been wandering those same hallways, but this time unlocking the prisons that hold people captive."

"That *does* sound good," he replied with a smile.

It is! And this isn't about whether people frequent a congregation or not. This is about feeling I had the responsibility to conform people to what I thought was best for them instead of freeing them to live in an affection-based relationship with God and letting *him* change *them*. I've never regretted that choice. And I've seen far more fruit rise from helping them live freely than I ever did from trying to get them to believe my conclusions or meet my expectations.

I don't try to convince anyone of anything anymore. I talk to hungry people about God's reality as I best understand it. When they are ready for it, they respond in ways that liberate them and invite them into the most transformative relationship the universe has to offer. When they aren't, I measure my words more carefully, seeking a way to love them rather than trying to set them straight. Only the Spirit can prepare them for the truth he wants to breathe into their lives. The more I try to convince them, the more I push them away from the light I want them to see. I want to treat them in a way that will invite them into the orbit of his love, where they will be better prepared to see through their deception and embrace what's true.

That's why love is the more excellent way. Without it, truth won't find its way in the world.

CHAPTER 23

· · · · · · · · · · · · · ·

INTENTIONALLY
RELATIONAL

I believe all those Scriptures about the body of Christ walking together in unity, encouraging each other daily, and sharing God's wisdom and presence to express a fuller portrait of who he is and how he works in the world. I believe in the power of cooperation and collaboration between those learning to live loved by the Father as a major way he makes himself known to the world around us. I am just not convinced that institutional programs and services are the only way to do that, and unfortunately are often an unwitting detriment to the very Scriptures they seek to fulfill.

The whole of Creation began inside a community of Father, Son, and Spirit celebrating life together and working for a common good. The trajectory of God's work in that Creation is to invite us to share in that community with him, and thus with each other. I am absolutely committed to sharing life inside the

Divine Community as much as I am able—both in my growing communion with the Godhead and in growing friendships with others who are learning to live there as well.

That's why I see church life not as an obligation, but as a vibrant treasure to be shared with delight. Each of us knows and sees in part, but the fullness of God's wisdom and nature can only be reflected as those pieces are brought together. While I get to express a facet of God's wonder, others around me express a different facet. As we walk together in love, the fullness of God's person becomes increasingly clear to us and to the world around us.

Unfortunately, the brokenness of our flesh and the politics inside our institutions seem to encourage us to treat each other more as competitors that collaborators. Threatened by the gifts of others and striving to brand our own names to build influence and market share, we pull apart more than we pull together. In doing so, we reflect more the spirit of this age than we do the Spirit of the Living God.

Having been both a participant and a leader in those institutions, I know that real community is more an illusion in those environments than it is a reality. We thought we could share the life of the church by simply attending the same meetings consistently. And in some ways we did, but only in limited ways and for brief seasons. The arc of our programs unwittingly drew people out of the very community we were hoping to build, and at times pitted us against each other in our differing hopes for the priorities and activities of the group. Too much of our energy and resources were taken up keeping the program running, and those who were supposed to protect us often exploited us for their own job security or to build their personal kingdom.

That's part of the reason why so many people are leaving the institutional form of church life. It may work for some, but an increasing number of people are looking for something more than being a spectator to whatever has been planned for them on stage. They find themselves thirsting for real community where authenticity is treasured, where encouragement and support come easily, and where it fits into our daily lives and doesn't just happen in a building far away.

Take away the building and the scheduled meetings, however, and some people lose their connection with others. They end up isolated and alone, claiming that they don't go to church, because they are the church. But we are not the church alone. We can be a part of his church, but the richness of its treasure is revealed by walking alongside others who stimulate our hearts to live more deeply in God's love and encourage us to trust him more.

Does such a church exist? Of course, she does, and she thrives in every nook and cranny of our world. She's growing in purity and brilliance and demonstrating to a broken world that the power of love is the greatest force in the universe. To find her we have to stop thinking of her as a "place" and see her as a "people." Wherever I've gone over the past twenty years, I've found her and the kind of relationships of self-sacrifice and affection that mark her presence. I've been deeply bonded to people from distant countries as well as to those around me.

Unfortunately, many centuries ago we started using the term "church" to describe institutions and denominations, many of which no longer demonstrate that reality. When we hear the term "church," we don't think of people who love each other in an "otherworldly" way, but of institutions that act just as every other human institution, often with a lot of political drama and too many broken relationships. We need to look past the marquee and the steeples that promise there's a church inside, and instead look for her in the relationships around us that are marked with Father's love and affection.

The only place I know to really share the community we see reflected in the Divine community is in ever-deepening friendships with others who are seeking to know him as well. Can that happen around preprogrammed meetings? Of course, it can, though it does so almost by accident. Friends don't grow by sitting in a meeting together weekly, but by seeking each other out during the week and finding the conversations that expose our hearts and reap the insights of others.

To experience that kind of life, however, we have to learn to live relationally, and that is less a matter of what meeting we attend as it is how free our heart is to engage others the way God engages us. And this is as true for those who have found a home in a traditional congregation as it is for those who are no longer there. Growing friendships is how this family connects and how it shares its life with the world, and that takes some intentionality on our part.

* * * * * *

Living Relationally on the Inside

What does it mean to live relationally? It means to live with an open, honest, compassionate heart toward people around you, whether they are followers of Christ yet or not. That may sound easy, but it is beyond your capabilities to do it. To love others like that we will first have to learn to live in the Father's love for us. There are no shortcuts here. Our fears and insecurities will make us relationally unavailable to others no matter how hard we will try to act otherwise. It takes time and healing for us to have the relational space to see others and care about them.

I've written in many other places about learning to live in that affection, most notably in *He Loves Me*, so I won't belabor it here other than to remind you that living loved by him is the first step to sharing that love with others. The more comfortable you get in his love, the freer you'll be to live relationally open to other people. If you need help learning how, this is a great place for relationship to begin. Ask someone you know who lives more deeply in his love to walk alongside you and help you learn to as well. A lot of good fellowship begins by seeking the input of others to find a way for you to live in his affection.

As you grow in that love you'll find your heart being increasingly open in ways that nurture great relationships, rather than, however unwittingly, pushing people away. So instead of trying to act relational, watch how God's love sets you increasingly free to engage others in fruitful ways. Here are some of the characteristics that I see in those who are learning to live freely in his love that encourage the kind of friendships that reflect the life of the church:

They value people, not for what you can get from them, but as fellow strugglers through the difficulties of life. These fellow strugglers provoke your compassion and are a repository of God's treasure, no matter how well-covered it might be under their brokenness. The desire to be alongside others in their joys and struggles will open doors to many relationships, and some of those will grow into real friendships.

They live inside their compassion.

For whatever reason, some people and circumstances grab at our hearts more than others. That doesn't mean those people are more valuable or more in need, only that God is inviting you into connection with them. You can't possibly engage everyone around you. When your heart is touched with someone else's situation, lean into the relationship as much as they will let you.

They live with integrity.

I am amazed at the number of people who use God's love as an excuse to be dishonest and to backstab others for their own gain. There's a reason why God seeks out those who are genuine and honest and why those people in our lives who demonstrate character and integrity mean the most to us. Growing trust in a relationship results from someone demonstrating trustworthiness, and without it, people will know we're just using them to fill our own needs.

They don't try to fix others.

Walking alongside someone means you're there as a resource for them, when they are ready. When you present yourself as an expert who can fix their problems, you'll already be shredding the environment in which real relationships grow. Be a soft place for them to land by being gentle and patient. Take an interest in them, and let them take an interest at their pace. Learn to recognize when others are getting defensive, and back off so as not to drive them deeper into the hole they are stuck in. Your love and grace will invite them out as God makes them ready.

They learn not to take offense.

Most people are quick to take offense and even assign motives they can't possibly know to someone else's actions. They storm off, hoping their pity-party will manipulate others to give them the attention they want. The people I know who are most connected to Jesus don't take offense easily, even at someone else's brokenness.

They can be reviled and come back loving, betrayed and still keep their heart open. When you get hurt, take it to Jesus and find out what unmet need in your own heart responds to people that way. That doesn't mean you have to let toxic people walk all over you, however. There is room for appropriate boundaries to people who act destructively. This is where you learn to live in your own freedom.

They share the bandwidth.

In almost every grouping, 20 percent of the people take up 80 percent of the bandwidth, and that's true on my social feeds as well. And I don't think that's just the difference between extrovert and introvert. Some people think their ideas and thoughts are what's most important and can't seem to leave room for other people. When you learn to love, you'll also learn to be a better listener and share the space for others. I used to be compelled to fill blank spaces, afraid that people would think nothing is happening, but in my travels, the best questions or observations almost always rise out of the silence, from someone who doesn't normally speak up easily. The space allows them to process and to risk.

They lose the need to compete.

When you feel yourself threatened by someone else's success, or fighting for a place in the conversation, you'll find yourself being more hurtful than helpful. When you trust God to make all the room for you that he wants, you won't need to push yourself on others, or try to outdo them in anything other than loving.

Certainly, these all represent a huge growth curve in our lives that takes years to bear fruit, so don't try to rush through all of these as techniques to learn. They are simply what a free and loving heart does when it is no longer twisted by its own ego or insecurities. When you think beyond groups, studies, and programmed activities, you'll engage people around you in a different way. You'll find yourself caring about them and their story. You'll engage them in conversation you both will find enjoyable and nurturing. This is as true for extroverts as introverts, though for introverts it will most likely involve fewer relationships that go far deeper.

* * * * * *

Living Relationally on the Outside

I know those who've left their congregation want to find people quickly to replace what they lost, but God wants to bring people into our lives more organically as we simply learn to live in his love and love the people he puts in front of us each day. The "need" for fellowship can actually be a deterrent to it, not only in seeing the doors God opens, but also in distorting the relationship with need before it simply becomes a friendship. Father knows what you need and how to bring people into our lives. I'm sure there are lots of folks around you to love and take an interest in. Loneliness is one of the great problems of our day, and there are no doubt lonely people around you looking for a friend.

That's what Jesus meant by leaving the ninety-nine for the one. If the people you know aren't hungry for relationships, find those who are. Often, you'll find these among the weak and marginalized in our social groupings. Those we consider "cool" often have a full load of friends, or, despite appearances, don't know how to be a friend, content to use people rather than care about them. Think less of who you'd like to befriend and more of those who would be blessed by your friendship.

God's Spirit is the one who best arranges the connections he wants for us. He knows the people in your area he wants you to walk with and when best to bring you together. I'd encourage you not to look so much for a group, but simply live in the reality of his love each day and love those he puts before you, even unbelievers, without trying to convince them to believe what you believe. Soon you'll find yourself in some interesting conversations about Jesus, and in time, surrounded with other folks on this journey. His body grows by these ever-expanding relationships, whether they already gather in a group or not.

Save space in your life for people. Busyness is often the result of insecurity that crams our lives beyond the margins so we feel productive, but we end up with no time to engage people in relaxed conversation where friendships can grow. If you don't create space for that, it won't just happen by chance. And these don't always have to be extra events. Look for ways to invite people into the routines of your day, like walking the dog, attending a Little League game, or doing a household project. Or better yet, share in theirs.

Make yourself available for new friendships that are not based on religious performance or the manipulations that go with it. They may be unbelievers even, but you can learn to love the people God already has before you—in your neighborhood, at work, or from chance meetings. Engage them in conversation, invite them over or out, and pursue those who seem to connect. The friendships that grow out of these connections will become a rich heritage in your own journey.

Sara and I sit down every week to talk and pray about the people God would want us to connect with that week, and when someone comes to mind, we're quick to pick up a phone or write an email to see if there's a need or a similar hunger on the other end. Sometimes we host a dinner party or BBQ and invite people we think would enjoy knowing each other.

If you're the kind of person who is able to open your life and home and help others make connections in this family, by all means do it. You don't need to organize a bunch of meetings. Just provide a place for people to connect and friendships to grow. Ninety percent of community happens over a meal, which can be as simple as bringing fast food to a park. As you're together, learn how to help people find their way into real conversations about their journeys and what they are learning. This is how community grows and helps others engage it as well.

Our ever-expanding friendships that revolve around the life and love of Jesus become a rich treasure trove of God's grace and wisdom. We can listen to God together and recognize more easily what he is saying or asking of us. We can support each other and collaborate together in sharing as we do what he asks. And we can pool our resources to help each other in time of need or help others around the world.

Being relational takes far more intentionality than organizing group activities and meetings, or attending them. The rewards, however, are far richer. As your friendships grow with others, you will find yourself in time surrounded by an ever-widening set of relationships that not only opens the door wider for you to discover more about God's wisdom and nature, but it also allows us to cooperate together, however he might ask us to share his glory in the world around us.

That's where the church becomes visible—not because we have a building on the corner, but because we love in a way that others want to embrace.

CHAPTER 24

. . . .

TO THE SAINTS
SCATTERED...

To the followers of Jesus scattered throughout the world, no longer attached to a specific congregation or denomination: Greetings from one of your kind and from Jesus himself. I pray this letter finds you growing in the affection of our Father, in the trust of his Son, and the wisdom and gentleness of his Spirit.

I know the way has not been easy. It never is for pioneers who move outside an established status quo in search of greater vitality and authenticity. I know most of you didn't plan to get here; you simply followed the hunger of your heart and his drawing of your conscience until you found yourself outside the circles you used to frequent and for a while found so helpful. Some of you got pushed out for asking the wrong questions; others just stopped going, wearied by the politics or how guilt and fear were used to keep people in line.

I have spent the last twenty years among those who have taken their liberty from Christianity-as-a-religion and yet continued to pursue a life in Christ as vibrant as the one he passed on to his disciples. Their journey beyond Sunday-morning Christianity only confirmed their choice. The people I admire most in this world are those who follow their spiritual hunger, even when it takes them beyond the comfort of their friends and family. Religion is built on approval needs, and when someone diverges from that conformity, they meet a host of well-intentioned, if not particularly sensitive, people trying to convince them they are wrong.

Jesus knows how painful your journey is better than anyone else. It is a road he walked as well. It is so easy to sing with great passion, "Though none go with me, still I will follow," and far more difficult to actually do it. When you do, however, I've no doubt it brings great joy to him, knowing the risk you took to follow him down an uncertain path. Live in that joy as you keep going, even if the road is more difficult than you imagined. Your pursuit will reward you in ways you maybe can't see yet, and fulfill the deepest hungers with his reality, his love, and his freedom.

I realize many of you need no encouragement from me. You have come to know Jesus and learned to follow him apart from the religious conventions of our culture, and are finding yourselves increasingly at rest in his provision and being fruitful for him where he has placed you. You have discovered that there is still a church in the world to connect with relationally that doesn't need the political gamesmanship or the mind-numbing routines of religion. I have met many of you around the world, and have been inspired by your courage to take the road less traveled and your resilience in the face of challenge, opposition, and false accusations.

Others of you are either new to the journey, or haven't settled into it yet. Here's what I've learned thus far into my journey:

* * * * * *

Finding A New Trailhead

The early days of living outside our systems of religious performance can be quite painful, depending on the reason you left and if you have some supportive voices around you. Initially, you'll feel great relief to be out of the situation that compelled you to make such a painful decision. You may have hoped others would have shared in your journey, and either come with you or be sympathetic to how God was leading you. Most people, however, find themselves outside alone where three critical challenges await, all of which also hold some great opportunities for growth.

Overcoming Guilt.

For a while you'll feel like you've lost your moorings, and your emotions will not be in sync with what you know to be true. You may know attendance at a congregation is not a requirement of our Lord Jesus, but you believed it for so long, and may have looked down on others who didn't come as regularly as you did, that you'll feel guilty when you're not there and defensive if people ask you about it.

Guilt is the acquired baggage of religious obligation. While we know that there is no longer any condemnation for those in Christ, it's amazing how much of our Christian experience has been driven by avoiding guilt and the disapproving glances of our fellow believers. It travels mostly unseen as long as you serve it, but when you stop, it rears its ugly head. Now you'll confront it

TO THE SAINTS SCATTERED...

head-on, almost every day, and it will test what you know about God, yourself, and what it means to follow him. This is a great time to see Jesus destroy the power guilt and fear hold over you.

You'll be tempted to do something to sate the guilt, or attack the systems others might enjoy, in order to justify your own experience. Resist those urges. This is an important time to find your way to the cross and discover the ways of thinking that create the guilt and condemnation you feel. As you lean more deeply into the Father's love and his wisdom, you'll find over time the guilt will lessen, as will your need to tear others down to feel good about his work in you.

Dealing with Loneliness.

If you were heavily involved in your local congregation you may have given it eight to ten hours per week, and it gave you the illusion that you were part of something larger than yourself. Even if friendships weren't as close as you'd hoped, you felt like you belonged, and that masked the loneliness that comes to the fore when you find yourself more isolated. Out of sight, out of mind is how most congregations work. People will miss your contributions more than they'll miss you.

Now you wonder if anyone was really a friend and does anyone care about you now. That is multiplied if you suffer the sting of judgment that comes if some of your closest friends and family begin to question your salvation, or at least view you as a reclamation project to get you back on the straight and narrow. It may even cause you to doubt that you're making the right choices.

That disappointment grows when new friendships or connections don't happen as fast as you hoped. Again, the temptation is to do something to fix the problem. Some seek out another congregation, try to find a house church near them, or even start their own. But the answer to your loneliness is not "out there" somewhere. It is not in a group you can find, a program you can institute, or a new guru to follow. You're not looking for a better way to do church, but a better way to embrace his reality. You will find loneliness first satisfied in him, and then it will spill into the relationships he will bring across your path.

You may not see it yet and you may even feel as if he has abandoned you, but he has not. He has not led you this far to forsake you, and he has not begun a work in you that he will not complete. This is the time to let your relationship with him deepen so you won't use others to fill the place only he can fill. This is a great season to learn how to seek him, to listen to him, and to follow him, and as you do, he will swallow up your loneliness in a vibrant communion with him. Then you're ready for healthier relationships in which true community can grow.

Losing Your Anger.

Departing a congregation is often laced with anger—at disappointed expectations, betrayal by people you thought loved you, or finally seeing through some of the false things you were taught to keep you loyal and contributing your time and resources. You'll want to blame people for lying to you or about you, and strike out against organized religion in general, falling prey to an us-versus-them dichotomy that will prove destructive over time.

This is all very natural to justify an extremely difficult decision you had to make and to navigate the self-doubt you will invariably experience. But you'll want to let it bleed out as soon as you can, which may still take months. Hopefully you can find a safe person who has been down this road before you to vent your pain with, without it overwhelming those who don't understand it and will only judge you for it.

In God's heart this journey is not about fixing "the church," but about drawing you into a deeper relationship with him and letting love, over time, still the anger of your heart and replace it with joy in his provision and compassion for others, even those who hurt you. This all may take years, so don't be hard on yourself if the emotions persist. Just keep leaning into him, and let his love win you out of feeling like someone else's victim. No, life isn't fair and people's failures will make your life more difficult, but he has a way to navigate you through all of that and give you the life that really is life. And keep in mind that your failures add difficulty to others as well.

Growing in him is a journey—its vitality will ebb and flow at times and there will be seasons where you'll get distracted, but when he makes you aware, guiltlessly lean back his direction.

A real relationship with him doesn't try to get from him what you want, but to receive what he wants to give you each day. Keep engaging him and don't pitch a tent anywhere thinking you've arrived. Our destination is not in this temporal age. Avoid simply falling into the routines of life and missing out on how this kingdom yearns to take shape in you—and through you find more space in the world.

If you have other believers around you who are on this journey, seek for their help in learning how to ignore guilt, satisfy your loneliness inside of Jesus, and to help you discover how to follow him as a real presence in your life. As you overcome these three challenges, you will find yourself on a very different journey.

* * * * * *

Settling into a Different Journey

Now you find yourself on a very different journey. Instead of meeting the expectations of the institution you belonged to, you may find yourself adrift without them. It was so easy when your security came from regular attendance, following the rules, speaking the party line, and gaining the approval from others for your diligent efforts. Without those you'll need to give attention to your connection with God himself. You will want to learn how to recognize his fingerprints in your day, and his words in the recesses of your thoughts.

Don't look for quick fixes here or rush the process. You cannot learn it in a book; you have to let it unfold in the reality of your circumstances. His curriculum is not in a workbook somewhere, or a university course; it is in the events, emotions, and thoughts of daily life as he comes alongside you to show you what's real and what is an illusion as you engage with his Spirit and the Scriptures.

Here are three things I use to keep my course:

Relational.

If you're new to this journey and still disoriented by the change from performance-based Christianity to an affectionate relationship with The Father, Jesus, and the Spirit, take all the time you need. Learn to let the Father enjoy your presence, and for you to enjoy his. If you need space from religious voices that seek to promote guilt and fear, take some distance from them. Jesus will show you who you are free to love, and what relationships draw you out of his affection and back into performance.

Eugene Peterson called it "the unforced rhythms of grace." Religious obligation and activity can so easily distract us from the purity and simplicity of how Jesus expresses himself to us. God already knows you and now wants you to know him. Jesus died to grant us full and confident access to him. It is not quick and it is not easy to learn how to live in that reality. He has to reshape internally the ways you were taught to live—twisted by indulging your desires, haunted by the insecurities of not knowing you were loved, exploited by the selfishness of others, or manipulated by the lies and fears of religious obligation.

Now he will teach you how to rest in his love, how your growing trust in his desires for you and his purpose in this age will change the way you navigate the world, and how your growing dependence on the power of his Spirit living in you will draw your eyes away from what's temporal to that which is eternal. Everything God wants to do in you, and all he wants to do through you, will grow naturally out of your engagements with him and the people he brings into your life.

If you can find them, spend time with others who stimulate awareness in your own life. Don't be discouraged if this takes some time or if that initially happens across great distances. Social media and blog comments might be a good place to connect as well, even if you can't be face-to-face. Beware the cheap fix of on-line networks or getting an identity from following a popular author or teacher. That may comfort you with a false security that will soon evaporate.

In time, you'll begin to meet people around you on a similar trajectory. Jesus is inviting an increasing number of people back to himself and creating a people who will follow the Lamb wherever he goes. You'll find those faster, however, if you're just looking for growing friendships with those already around you, not by finding or building a group of like-minded people. Keep your eyes open for a hungry seeker at work, an open-hearted neighbor, someone you meet randomly, or a person you connect with at another gathering or mission outreach. Fellowship grows from friendships a lot easier than friendship grows from meetings.

Truth-full.

Don't just throw out the illusions without rethinking where God's truth lies. Deconstructing the false messages of religion that feed performance and destroy community is a painful process. Not everyone survives it with a passion for truth. Once you find out some of the things you were taught aren't true, it's easy to throw out everything or just hold on to those things that you find personally comforting. Many have taken this course into the theological weeds and gotten lost in the skepticism about God and his truth.

Truth will often disturb us before it sets us free. Scripture underlines how hungering for truth is the most important component to grasping it. Don't seek voices who say what you want to be true; ask the Father to reveal his truth to you. Search your heart, search the Scriptures, and interact with others in conversation and through books and articles in a way that will help you reconstruct an understanding of who God truly is and his purpose in the world. God didn't bring you out of religious performance to leave you drifting on the winds of circumstance, but to draw you into a relationship that is not only intimate but transforming.

You won't have all the answers, and you'll lose your need to convince others that you see it better than they do. You'll learn to walk with him in the truth that is sometimes challenging and painful, but it will always draw your heart more closely to him. Don't expect this truth to be as much measured by principles you can follow, but in learning to discern in your unfolding day which decisions lead to life and which lead to death. This is where he always wanted to write his will—not in precepts to follow, but in learning to sense the pleasure of the Spirit in the direction he desires for us, and the restlessness of the Spirit when he's drawing us away from our own selfishness. That's how you learn to walk with him.

Purposeful.

When you are part of a religious program, everything is provided for you. You have fellowship because you sit in a congregation, worship because you sing, and spread the kingdom because your congregation gives to overseas missions. But those are simply shadows of a greater reality. To embrace those realities, now you will need to make some intentional choices to follow his leadings, embrace his purpose in circumstances around you, and to live focused more on others than yourself.

It is easy for all of us to drift into complacency regarding spiritual realities. Life takes so much out of us just to complete our job responsibilities and care for our families. It also distracts us with too many entertainment options, so that it's easy to end up coasting spiritually into emptiness. Growing in him and flowing with his purpose won't happen by accident, but it also won't happen by human ingenuity. I realize that sounds like a contradiction. What you will want to do is to learn to live in the moment, with a growing trust in Spirit's ability to lead and guide you. Being intentional is not doing what we prefer or even think best, but to see where love leads us and where his Spirit nudges us.

When you stop serving someone else's vision it will be easier to recognize his leading. Let him grow your capacity to love so that you'll have a heart of compassion for the broken, and be a champion of justice for the oppressed. Confront evil where it exploits the innocent, quickly repair broken relationships where possible with forgiveness and honesty, and treat others the way you want them to treat you.

Walking by the Spirit comes with a suspicious eye toward our own human effort, but an intentional eye on the Father and flowing with his activity in the world.

* * * * * *

Helping Others Find Their Journey

The time is coming when all that you've discovered will not just be valuable for you, but will overflow from you to so many others who are hungering for the same realities that lie beyond the walls of their own experience. Jesus designed his kingdom to work that way. As freely as you receive, you look for ways to freely give to others. As you find more relaxed footing in your relationship with him, look for ways to be a blessing to others.

I'm convinced this is what it means to pastor the flock of God. It doesn't require a degree or a job managing an institution; it is simply the ability and desire to help others connect with Jesus and encourage them as they learn to follow him. God works through the simplest people who have sincere hearts, not those who seek visibility on the stage. Sharing your life freely is not a task you have to do, but one that will flow out of your heart naturally as you make yourself available to him.

Live lovingly.

What I enjoy most about this journey is that all the obligations and expectations I lived under were replaced with a sense of endearment. I don't follow God because I'm afraid of him, but because I want what he wants for me. I don't do what I do in fear that he will punish me, but because I want to share in the work he is doing around me. Obligation was replaced with joy, and though I can't stop and love everyone I pass on a given day, I've always got an eye out for the person God wants me to engage or to serve in some way.

Live freely.

There will be no end of well-meaning people who will want to push their preferences and expectations on you. You can be gracious as you politely say, "No, thank you." Embrace what God gives you, and turn from those things others want to force on you. Life is too short to let people manipulate you, even with the best of their religious intentions. You are to live to him, free from the tyranny of your own spiritual ambitions, and free from others' as well.

Live generously.

Keep an eye out for the needs and welfare of others, sharing whatever you might have to be a blessing in someone else's life. Build friendships and share those friendships with others by connecting people who will be blessed to know each other. This is how his church grows in the world. Don't just love those who can love you back, but take time with people who do not yet have any capacity for love, so that they can see him in you.

Live genuinely.

No one needs you to pretend to be someone you're not, or further down the road than you are. We best help people when we let them look into the reality of our lives to see both where God has shaped his life in us and where we still struggle. Impress people with your honesty, not by pretending to be further down the road than you really are. Sharing your own doubts and failures are as important as telling others how God makes himself known to you. None of us has it all together, and authenticity laced with humility creates the vulnerable environment where the best conversations happen. It will free you to love and to honesty without the need to fix others or make them part of your agenda.

Live justly.

Life is inherently unfair and it is somehow in the nature of powerful people to exploit others for their own gain and notoriety. The kingdom comes to bind up the brokenhearted, to free the oppressed, and to help the poor and downtrodden. Keep an eye out for those whom the culture exploits and be a champion for compassion and justice. Don't make conformity the currency of relationship, but care and concern. You cannot love all the people in the world, so love well those God puts before you each day.

* * * * * *

In Christ Alone

Jesus is doing an amazing thing in our day: he is taking his church back. He's calling people from every corner of this world to find him as their sole allegiance. Some of those are inside traditional congregations, and many others he is inviting outside to teach them another way to live and grow.

The truth be told, we are all part of the saints scattered, even those who regularly attend a local congregation. The saints have been scattered for a long time, divided by institutions, doctrines, leaders, and programs, each believing their way is the best. For those of us who have moved beyond Sunday gatherings as the focus of our faith, we need to take care that we guard our hearts to explore the wonder of the whole body of Christ as she is in the world. Almost every group that has splintered off of Christian institutions in the past has gone on to create their own, looking down on those who didn't live it the same way they did.

It would seem that the courage it takes to leave religious obligation easily bends toward pride and an air of superiority if we're not careful. Yes, our institutional systems can be deeply flawed as they try to express God's reality in the world, but that doesn't mean we need to condemn them or think less of those who attend them. Our world is touched for the better by many of those congregations. Though it may not be the best way for your hungers to be met, resist the desire to reject others who see it differently. Don't think your path is their path or that those not on it can't know and follow the God you're growing to know. He has many sheep and he does not lead all on the same path.

Always keep in mind that it is Jesus' desire to reconcile *all* things to himself, and thus all of us to each other. This is the unity he prayed for with such passion. That we would all be one, as he and the Father are one. We have too long looked for that to come from our institutions or our agreed-upon doctrines, but that approach has failed us spectacularly. The unity Jesus prayed for can only come through transformed lives as we let God's kind of love permeate our own hearts and free us to live with increasing selflessness and generosity in a world that knows too little of either.

Give yourself to what leads to authentic unity. Remember, this is his work, not yours, so be patient and don't think you will have to compromise his work in you to love others who are on a different journey. Don't be afraid to follow your heart, and encourage others to follow theirs as well. While you will often be judged maliciously, don't resolve your pain by judging back. Bring those accusations to God and leave them there. If he is not asking you to change, don't let others press you towards it.

Let all kinds of people into your life to see what loving them might do. Those who criticize how you live your life may not be against the Jesus we love and seek to follow. Don't exalt yourself because God has given you more to see; instead, use it as a way to serve others so that they will have a chance to see it, too.

This is the trajectory he invites all his children on, and if it has taken you outside the walls of institutionalism, it was not to separate you from his people, but to draw you more deeply into the life that truly is life and to free you to share that love without any borders. His purpose was not to leave you isolated and scattered in the world, but increasingly transformed by love so that he can knit you into the fabric of his church as she is taking shape around the world today.

And she is taking shape in ways most people miss. Wherever I travel in the world, I meet people who are really learning to live a journey in Christ that is transforming them from the need to serve themselves and to a more generous heart for others. These are the stories that thrill my soul and give me hope. They are being led by Jesus, often in direct contradiction to their own self-interest. Soon they will be knit together by his Spirit in ways we cannot yet conceive, but will speak of his glory far more than our own ingenuity.

Let's take care that we do not exalt anything above Christ and Christ alone, the hope of glory for every individual. Don't give people a reason to be distracted by your pet doctrines, cute terminology, or a specific program that may have been useful for you but may not be for them. Focus on him and his reality, and watch him reveal himself in almost every relationship you have. Don't fragment his family because you want to make a name for yourself, to brand an identity, or to carve off a market share for your ministry.

Share freely as God cares for you. Yearn for the day when we will be truly one flock with one Shepherd. As long as we have other humans between us and our compassionate High Priest, we will continue to live in splintered, discordant factions. The world is not surprised by such.

But imagine what it would think if they really saw the followers of Christ loving each other deeply, from the heart. There he will be revealed in ways that will draw the most calloused sinner to recognize who he is. And then we won't be scattered anymore, but one body permeating every corner of our world with the life and love of Jesus.

To find out more about Wayne's writings, teachings, and travel, you can find him at Lifestream.org and TheGodJourney.com

LIFESTREAM
1560-1 Newbury Rd. #313
Newbury Park, CA 91320
(805) 498-7774
office@lifestream.org

If you want help exploring your own relationship with Jesus, Wayne has designed some free resources to help you get a handle on your own journey. They are available at Lifestream.org and can be utilized individually or shared as small group exercises.

TRANSITIONS: An eight-hour audio series to help you break free of religious obligation and find your way into an affection-based relationship with God.

ENGAGE: A series of six- to eight-minute videos to help you recognize how God is already building a relationship with you.

THE JESUS LENS: A nine-hour video series to help you read the Scriptures through the revelation of Jesus instead of the religious lenses that have distorted its message.

THE GOD JOURNEY: A weekly podcast to encourage people on a more relational journey.

You can also find Wayne's other books, audio collections, and DVD series at Lifestream.org.

· · · · · · · · · · · · ·

ACKNOWLEDGMENTS

This book has been a lifetime in the making. Truly, to do justice to this page, I'd have to thank everyone whose life somehow made an impact on my own over many years. That is, literally, almost everyone I've ever met. I couldn't be more grateful at this stage of my life for the journey God has given me and the people who played a role in that, even those whose brokenness added pain to my own journey. It is clear to me now that times of pain have done more to challenge and reshape my own journey than moments of ease and comfort.

Since it would be impossible to list everyone I could include above, let me express my thanks to those most close at hand who have paid a great price to walk this journey alongside me. Sara, my wife of nearly forty-three years, has lived all of this with me, and none of what I have learned would have happened without her willingness to travel with me, even through uncertain seasons. Her love, support, and partnership have made my life rich beyond anything I would have imagined, and she has helped me see God's wisdom more clearly. My children Julie and Andrew have also brought great joy to my life as they have found their own journeys and always loved and supported me no matter what. And, of course, to my son-in-law Tyler and those three incredibly delightful grandchildren, Aimee, Lindsay, and Austin, who bring such joy to life.

The conversations I had with Brad Cummings on a podcast called *The God Journey* helped solidify so many of the thoughts contained in this book. His friendship over the past stretch of my life has enriched and challenged me to think beyond my first impulses and see into a larger world.

The skills and talents of Abigail Munday and Nan Bishop provided the practical help I needed to bring this book together. Abigail took over copyediting duties when my regular editor was unavailable. I appreciate her hard work in making this a more readable manuscript. Nan Bishop of N Bishop Designs (www.nbishopsdesigns.com) worked out the cover with me and the inside layout. They not only do great work, but share my passion for the life of Jesus unfolding in the earth.

Finally, I want to acknowledge the board of Lifestream Ministries, dear friends without whose support and wisdom I could not have explored some of the roads less traveled. I appreciate their humor and insight as they have helped me discern the Lord's leading instead of getting me to fulfill their expectations.